Scotland's Hidden History

Scotland's Hidden History

Ian Armit

The
History
Press

For Catriona

First published in 1998 by Tempus Publishing
New edition published in 2006

Reprinted in 2009 by
The History Press
The Mill, Brimscombe Port,
Stroud, Gloucestershire, GL5 2QG
www.thehistorypress.co.uk

Reprinted 2011

British Library Cataloguing in Publication Data.
A catalogue record for this book is available from the British Library.

ISBN 978 0 7524 3764 4

Typesetting and origination by
Tempus Publishing Limited
Printed and bound in Great Britain by
Marston Book Services Limited, Didcot

Contents

List of Illustrations

The cover illustration, of The Ring of Brodgar, Orkney, is reproduced by courtesy of Historic Scotland.

COLOUR PLATES

TEXT FIGURES

Preface to the
Second Edition

The original edition of this book appeared in 1998. The publication of this revised edition has enabled me to make some significant changes. The most important is the updating and revision of the bibliography. Archaeological research has moved on considerably even in the eight years between editions, and it is remarkable how many new publications have appeared in that time. Elsewhere the changes are less radical. Most new research focuses on excavation, often in the arable lowlands, where the sorts of sites encountered do not lend themselves to permanent preservation and are thus unlikely to knock the prime visitor monuments off their pedestals. There are of course exceptions, the most obvious recent example being the extraordinarily well-preserved broch complex of Old Scatness in Shetland, which I have built into the pre-existing entry for Jarlshof. I have updated other individual site entries where appropriate, but the main changes have been in the introductory sections of each chapter where the impact of recent work can be most easily accommodated.

As before, I would like to thank all those who read and commented upon the text of both this and the previous edition: Patrick Ashmore, Gordon Barclay, Dr David Breeze, Dr Noel Fojut, Catriona Armit and Professor Ian Ralston. Flaws which remain are entirely the author's responsibility.

I am also grateful to the following friends and colleagues for their help at various stages of the work: Mike Brooks, Kirsty Cameron, David Henrie, Fraser Hunter, Richard Langhorn, Dr Anna Ritchie, Ian Shepherd, Joe White, and Caroline Wickham Jones. Peter Kemmis Betty and Dr David Breeze provided help and encouragement throughout.

The author and publisher would also like to thank the following for permission to reproduce illustrations: Historic Scotland (*24, 28-9, 35, 39, 45, 55, 58, 61, 66, 68-9,*

71-3, 79, 82, 84, 86-7 and all colour plates except 2, 12, 13 and 19), Museum nan Eilean (3, 56, 62), The Trustees of the National Museum of Scotland (8, 10, 11), the Royal Commission on the Ancient and Historical Monuments of Scotland (6-7, 12, 25, 27, 30, 32, 34, 36, 37-8, 41, 44, 47-8, 50-2, 57, 60, 63, 65, 67, 70, 76-8, 80-1 and colour plates 12, 13 and 19), Ian Shepherd and Aberdeenshire Council (40). Historic Scotland provided support for the production of maps and original drawings.

The reconstruction drawings and regional maps are by Alan Braby with the exceptions of 20 (Kirsty Cameron), 59 (Alan Sorrell), and 68-9 (MJ Moore). The front cover photograph is by David Henrie.

How to use this book

The chapters are structured to provide a narrative account of Scotland's past, using each individual monument to illustrate the main themes. Each monument has its own entry, with instructions on how to get there. Each entry also gives the national grid reference (NGR) so that the map-literate reader can track down the exact location, particularly on the 1:50,000 Ordnance Survey Landranger maps. The bracketed number after each site identifies the location of the site on the map at the beginning of each chapter. Finally, there is a brief guide to the archaeological literature, and lists of museums and heritage attractions with collections and displays relevant to the themes of the book.

Most of the sites mentioned are in public ownership, a great many of them in the care of Historic Scotland. More information on these, for example regarding opening hours, can be obtained from Historic Scotland, Longmore House, Salisbury Place, Edinburgh, EH9 1SH. For those sites on private land, please always remember to ask permission before entering, be sure to close gates etc., and leave the site as you found it.

I

Introduction:
Scotland to AD 1000

People have lived in Scotland for at least 10,000 years, for the first 9000 of which no recognisable concept of 'Scotland' even existed. Most books on Scottish history dispose of this first 9000 or so years in a curt preliminary chapter, before moving on to the more familiar kings, queens, barons and battles that populate Scottish medieval history.

There are good reasons for this approach. Before AD 1000 written records are sparse and often uninformative. Before the first century AD they are non-existent. The bulk of evidence for human history in this period comes rather from the archaeology.

While historians of later periods have the security of their written documents, archaeologists have to deal with a rather different, and often cripplingly limited set of data. Their evidence often seems unpromising: broken tools, scraps of pot, lost or buried jewellery, pollen trapped in peat bogs, and the denuded shells of long abandoned buildings, all seem unlikely sources of historical knowledge. Indeed, when it comes to answering many of the questions of conventional history, they are hopeless. We can never recover the names of prehistoric people, tribes or societies, or understand the actions or motives of particular individuals or groups. Our attempts at understanding usually have to be pitched at a broader scale: economic, technological and social change over centuries or millennia rather than years or decades.

Yet some archaeological answers are unambiguous. The prehistoric past was far from a primitive timeless idyll, waiting to be kicked into consciousness by the spread of written documents. From the introduction of agriculture, and probably long before, societies constantly evolved, interacted and changed. Economies and technologies were periodically revolutionised, social relationships between individuals and social classes were often in a state of flux, and the nature of religious belief and practice was seldom static. Changes in each of these spheres can be detected and demonstrated through archaeology, as can the considerable changes that prehistoric communities wrought on the landscapes of Scotland.

Neither did the processes of change always work in one direction. Although there was a gradual development of new and more effective technologies over many millennia, this was not reflected by any unflinching march of social evolution. Social complexity seems to have varied a great deal from period to period and area to area .

The following chapters tell the story of Scotland before AD 1000, as we understand it today, through some of the most important surviving monuments. While the text draws upon all the archaeological evidence available, including the results of excavation, individual objects, and aerial photography, it is through visiting these monuments and examining their fragile remains that some flavour may be recaptured of the past cultures and societies that inhabited what is now Scotland. Firstly, though, it may be useful to give a brief overview of our present understanding.

HUNTER GATHERERS (8000 BC − 4000 BC)

Although Britain was occupied as early as 500,000 years ago, traces of the first visitors and colonists in Scotland are unknown until after the last glaciation (1). It seems unlikely that this represents a genuine avoidance of the north during earlier periods; more probably the very earliest settlements were simply scoured away by the invading ice. Traces of settlement from this period (the Palaeolithic, or 'Old Stone Age') may yet be found in sheltered locations such as caves, if these were inhabited at the time, but for now the earliest known settlers arrived at a rather less distant period.

The first clear evidence for the presence of people in Scotland dates to around 7500 BC. This is the period known to archaeologists as the Mesolithic (or 'Middle Stone Age'). As elsewhere in the temperate forested lands of northern and western Europe, these communities lived by exploiting a diverse range of natural resources. They relied heavily on wild plant foods, such as fruit, nuts, seeds and roots, and on the hunting of wild animals, such as red deer, boar and small mammals. Over much of Scotland, as at all periods of its later history, fishing would have been crucial.

The areas most favoured for settlement seem to have been the coastal zone and the main river valleys where a range of wild resources was available. Occasionally Mesolithic communities gave nature a helping hand by deliberately starting forest fires to create clearings where wild animals would congregate to graze.

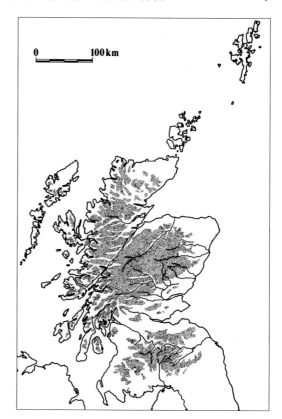

1 Scotland

Generally, however, these people meddled much less with their environment than any subsequent inhabitants of Scotland.

Since wild foods would often have been seasonal and thinly spread, Mesolithic communities generally lived in small bands and moved around a great deal, perhaps on an annual cycle (*2*). The country would not have been particularly densely settled, but by around 10,000 years ago most of it, including the islands of the north and west, had probably already been occupied.

THE FIRST FARMERS (4000 BC – 2000 BC)

Signs of a major change in the nature of these hunting and gathering societies in Scotland came around 4000 BC, with the first appearance of farming communities (in the archaeological period known as the Neolithic or 'New Stone Age'). Farming seems to have had its origins in the Near East, where the wild ancestors of the early domesticated animals and cultivated plants are found. Once a knowledge of farming had spread to south-western Europe, however, it rapidly expanded northwards and westwards along the major river valleys that dissect the continent, along with a

2 Artist's reconstruction of a Mesolithic camp

series of assorted cultural traits with which it had become associated. These included pottery, polished stone axes, elaborate houses and enclosures.

By the time this 'wave of advance' reached the north and west fringes of Europe, however, it appears to have stalled. While the communities who lived in these areas adopted some aspects of the material culture associated with farming, notably pottery, they seem to have retained much of their traditional way of life for many centuries before their final adoption of farming. By the time knowledge of farming, pottery manufacture and other new cultural traits reached Scotland, they had thus been filtered through many generations of communities not too dissimilar from the indigenous Mesolithic inhabitants. We need not expect, therefore, that the adoption of farming in Scotland constituted a particularly sudden economic or social revolution (3). It probably happened in different ways and at different rates in different parts of Scotland.

This apparent stutter on the path of human progress may appear initially surprising but it is easy to forget that farming has no inherent immediate advantage over hunting and gathering as a means of subsistence. The Mesolithic communities of Scotland would not have seen agriculture as a necessary first step towards cities, writing and space travel, but rather as a potentially risky investment of time and labour in activities quite alien to their own cultural traditions and possibly to their social or spiritual beliefs. The real reasons for the eventual adoption of farming may lie less in the inherent attractions of agricultural drudgery and more in the demands of existing social practices for exotic products such as crops and domestic animals for feasting and gift-giving. Some new settlers may also have arrived to farm under-used areas, perhaps those which were less suited to the Mesolithic lifestyle but quite acceptable for new agricultural economies.

3 Artist's reconstruction of Neolithic farming around Calanais stones

The adoption and spread of farming eventually dictated a basically settled lifestyle, binding people to the land on which they lived and depended. It created, perhaps for the first time, a situation where communities could invest time and energy in the construction of permanent settlements, and strengthened the bond between the community and its territory. It also, importantly, opened up tremendous potential for population expansion, since communities could now extract more food from a given patch of land by the application of more labour; a facility that their hunting and gathering ancestors entirely lacked. The associated clearance of woodland for agriculture, and the spread of grasslands for grazing, set about the serious process of human modification of the natural landscape that continues even today.

TOMBS AND TEMPLES (4000 BC – 2000 BC)

Despite their new settled lifestyle it is little easier to detect the houses of these new farmers than those of their more mobile ancestors. Indeed the Neolithic period is characterised less by houses and fields than by temples and tombs. This may be because Neolithic houses (with some notable exceptions discussed in Chapter 2) were often fairly slight constructions, built of timber, turf and earth; or perhaps communities continued to move around, albeit within a smaller area of land, and needed little more than easily portable skin tents or other ephemeral constructions for shelter. In comparison to the fugitive remains of their houses, however, there is a veritable profusion of Neolithic burial monuments of all shapes and sizes; known generically as chambered tombs (*4*). The homes of the dead were a great deal more visible than the homes of the living.

4 A Neolithic chambered tomb: Barpa Langass in North Uist

The discrepancy of scale and permanence between houses and tombs is by no means peculiar to Scotland. In some parts of Europe, the architecture of tombs even seems to echo that of contemporary houses, transformed from perishable earth and timber to monumental stone.

These chambered tombs were not simple burial vaults. The bones they contained were often heavily abraded and sorted, suggesting that the bodies had been subject to prior burial or exposure, and that the bones may have been periodically used in subsequent rituals and ceremonies. Clearly, the ancestors were an important commodity to the first farmers, and played a significant role in their world view.

Although the stone monuments of the north and west of the country are among the most obvious today, the east and south saw the construction of similar structures from less durable materials, such as timber, earth and turf. Although they have weathered and eroded much more than their stone counterparts, their sheer mass means that many of these round mounds and long barrows can still be seen.

The earliest tombs seem to have been burial places of relatively small, local communities, built and used over many generations. The Neolithic period, however, also saw the emergence of great communal monuments that must have brought together quite large groups of people for their construction. These included elongated enclosures known as cursus monuments, and then later stone circles and henges (large circular enclosures which take their name from Stonehenge). These were clearly not standard farming settlements or places of defence and, although some people were buried on these sites, burial was not their prime purpose. Instead, the available evidence suggests that they were of deep religious significance, apparently associated with the observation and veneration of the sun, moon and stars.

While there is no sign in the earlier part of the Neolithic period of high-ranking chiefs, priests or other individuals with great personal wealth, the situation changed in the later part of the period when these communal structures were being built. Monuments on this scale imply the presence of people with the authority to demand and marshall the labour of whole communities. Pottery styles show startling similarities from Orkney to Wessex, suggesting that at least some of these people, whether chiefs, priests, or some combination of the two, had extensive contacts and were able to move around a great deal.

SETTLEMENT EXPANSION AND THE RISE OF THE INDIVIDUAL (2000 BC − 700 BC)

From around 2000 BC, the great communal monuments of the Neolithic began to be abandoned or altered. Some were even commandeered to build burial mounds for single individuals. There was, it seems, a major switch in emphasis away from communal burial and worship to the glorification of the individual by elaborate single burial.

This period also saw the adoption of bronze, at first mainly for decorative items, but increasingly thereafter for tools and weapons. This new technology demanded closer contacts between disparate communities, since the necessary copper and tin ores that are combined to make bronze seldom occur together.

Societies at this time, or at least their most prosperous members, seem to have exchanged prestigious exotic goods as gifts, tribute or bride-wealth, and these objects were often moved over great distances, perhaps through several changes of owner. Ownership of these 'prestige goods' seems to have become symbolic of social power.

It seems then that, at the dawn of the Bronze Age, the old religious hierarchies of the Neolithic had been eased out of power by a new secular aristocracy which paid greater attention to individual status than to the worship of celestial deities or the ancestors. Certainly, ritual expression had changed by the latter centuries of the second millennium BC. While the old temples were largely abandoned, rich sacrifices of portable wealth, such as bronze weapons, were now offered up in rivers, pools and bogs, or buried underground. Some have suggested that even the nature of the gods themselves changed: the sky gods, worshipped at the earlier henges and stone circles were replaced by gods of the earth or underworld worshipped in these new rites.

At more or less the same time as the adoption of bronze in Scotland, a new style of ceramic, known as beaker pottery, came to prominence across much of northern and western Europe. Beaker pottery comprised a range of fairly small, fine drinking vessels usually profusely decorated. Very often these vessels are found carefully placed in graves along with a variety of other grave goods, including jewellery, weapons and items associated with archery (5).

The spread of this new pottery tradition was once seen as reflecting the movement of a 'Beaker Folk', who were thought to have invaded and colonised much of Europe, displacing the native inhabitants. Yet the manifest continuity in other aspects of material culture in these areas lends little credence to this view. It seems more likely that beaker pottery was adopted as part of new quasi-religious rites associated with drinking, or simply the introduction and spread of alcohol. Some Scottish beakers found in graves certainly seem to have held mead or beer for the deceased to quaff in the afterlife.

Through the centuries 2000-1000 BC other great changes took place that may have had more significance for the daily lives of most people in Scotland than the varying styles of pottery prevalent among the social elite. Settlement seems to have spread well into the uplands in areas such as Sutherland and Perthshire, reaching altitudes that would be unthinkable for arable farming today (6). Clearly the gentler climate of that time was a factor, but population expansion and improved farming techniques must have played a part.

The density of farming settlement in the uplands is known only because of the avoidance of these areas by destructive later agriculture. In these marginal and unproductive lands, hundreds of prehistoric ro undhouses together with their sprawling irregular fields, testify to the tenacity of prehistoric farming communities. In the lowlands, subject to intensely destructive agriculture over countless generations, few such traces are visible above ground. Yet these areas must surely have been farmed to capacity before the colonisation of the uplands was even contemplated.

Some of these upland outposts of Bronze Age agriculture were destined to be fairly short-lived. Climatic deterioration, combined with soil exhaustion and erosion through over-cultivation, led in some areas, such as Sutherland, to the abandonment of many upland farms before the end of the second millennium BC. The dense dust clouds thrown into the atmosphere as a by-product of volcanic activity in Iceland may have been a further contributory factor in worsening the climate at this time. Such effects, however, were probably not felt across the whole country.

FORTS AND FARMS (1000 BC − AD 80)

In the centuries following 1000 BC society seems to have become rather more inward-looking. Instead of prestige goods and widespread social contacts, more importance seems to have been attached to the locality and the home, with

Right: 5 A typical beaker
assemblage

Below: 6 A landscape of
prehistoric settlement
remains in upland
Perthshire

communities devoting much of their energies to enclosure and defence (which, as we shall see, could be as much symbolic as practical). Burial or overtly religious sites are extremely rare for this period (*8*).

For the first time, in this period, we see the emergence of heavily enclosed and defended settlements taking a whole variety of forms. These range from a handful of very large agglomerations of settlement, holding hundreds of houses, to small settlements of a couple of houses surrounded by a timber stockade. The control over land expressed by the imposing physical presence of such structures seems to mark the emergence of a new territorial awareness (*7*).

One reason for the breakdown of wider contacts, and the relatively cosmopolitan outlook of the Later Bronze Age, seems to have been the introduction of iron around 700 BC and the consequent decline of the bronze industry. Since iron could often be obtained locally, the elaborate networks that had grown up around the trade in bronze soon became obsolete. Those whose power and prestige had been founded on their control of exchange and bronze production lost their hold over society, and power seems to have become somewhat diffused as communities became more self-sufficient in metal production.

While the dense spreads of forts and enclosures across much of Scotland may be one manifestation of the collapse of the Bronze Age hierarchies and the greater autonomy of smaller territorially-minded groups, another may be

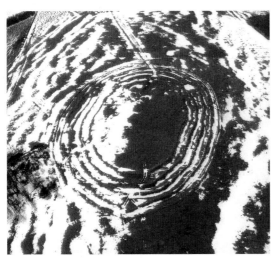

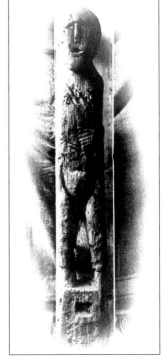

Above: 7 An Iron Age hillfort: Corsehope Rings in the Borders

Right: 8 This life-size wooden idol was recovered from a peat bog at Ballachulish in 1880. It dates to around 600 BC and gives a vivid impression of the wealth of Iron Age material lost through natural decay

represented by the appearance of monumental roundhouses. The best known of these are the broch towers of the north and west, but timber versions in the south and east were perhaps equally impressive and probably more numerous. Artificial islets, or crannogs, represent yet another expression of the same phenomenon of monumental roundhouse building that characterised the Iron Age across much of Britain from Wessex to Shetland (9).

The fragmented societies that seem to have characterised the middle centuries of the first millennium BC did not remain static. Indeed, by the latter centuries BC there are some signs that larger tribal groups were beginning to form again. Huge inroads seem to have been made in clearing the remaining woodlands of the south and east, enabling the spread of farming into the uplands, while some lowland areas were divided up by massive field complexes. The scale of these works is such that some organising force must surely have been in operation.

By now, most of the old hillforts lay abandoned and the majority of people seem to have lived in open settlements of small timber roundhouses. A proliferation of large grain stores, known as souterrains, seems to suggest that the communities of eastern Scotland were by now producing a significant arable surplus which required centralised storage, again hinting at stable conditions and powerful leaders. The appearance of nucleated villages based around some of the northern broch towers might herald the emergence of similarly successful rulers in the far north.

It is to this society that the many fine objects in a style known as La Tène or Early Celtic Art originally belonged. Prestige items such as body armour, helmets and horsegear, often in bronze, were embellished with elaborate and flowing curvilinear ornament of a kind found across much of Europe. These objects not only highlight the presence of a social elite with militaristic aspirations, but also of a well-provisioned class of craftworkers whose knowledge and skills tied them into pan-European cultural and artistic traditions. There are occasional hints too of religious practices, such as the veneration of the human head, and the use of certain ritual artefacts, that suggest the presence of a priestly class broadly equivalent to the druids described by Caesar in Gaul, Wales and England.

THE ROMAN INTERLUDE (AD 80 – AD 400)

The adoption of Early Celtic art styles by the tribal leaders of Scotland in the last couple of centuries BC is one of the few archaeological signs that these people were being drawn back into contacts with their peers in other parts of Britain and Europe, probably for the first time in several centuries. Yet, even by this time, these related groups were, one by one, succumbing to the power of the advancing Roman Empire, which was to introduce wholly new political and cultural forces into native societies across much of northern and western Europe.

9 Artist's reconstruction of an Iron Age crannog

Around AD 80, after a generation or more of conquest and consolidation in what is now England, the Roman army finally entered Scotland and embarked upon the first in a long series of bloody but ultimately inconclusive military campaigns (*10*). Lying at the very limits of an Empire stretching south to Egypt, west to Portugal, and east to Mesopotamia, Scotland was never fully assimilated by Rome: its full conquest seems never to have been sufficiently pressing for the proper resources to be provided.

Nonetheless, the archaeological legacy of this Roman interlude is extremely rich, although formed almost exclusively of military constructions of one sort or another. Forts, fortlets, signal stations and temporary camps proliferate in many parts of the south and east, while the extensive road network and successive frontier systems (including the Antonine Wall) carved up the native landscape on a wholly unprecedented scale.

There was no unified native response to the Roman presence. Certain tribal groups, particularly the Votadini in the south-east, may have positively welcomed the invaders and probably appreciated the havoc wrought on their northern neighbours while their own territory remained apparently unmolested and ungarrisoned (*11*). The tribes of the north-east, by contrast, seem to have posed far greater problems for the Roman army as witnessed by the dense spread of Roman military installations, and the periodic punitive campaigns of successive Emperors.

Although there was nothing even approximating to a 'national struggle' against the Roman army, the disruptions of this period seem to have been accompanied by a gradual amalgamation of the disparate Iron Age tribes beyond the Empire into larger power blocks. While early Roman sources, collated by the geographer Ptolemy, listed 12 tribes north of the Forth, around 100 years later only the Caledonians and the Maeatae rated a mention. Early in the next century Cassius Dio, writing of the Caledonians, states that 'the names of the others have been included in these'. By the fourth century AD an even larger unit known as the Picts had emerged, seemingly as a growing confederacy of the Caledonians and other tribes.

POST-ROMAN PEOPLES (AD 400 – AD 1000)

By the middle of the millennium, the Roman Empire had receded from Britain and the descendants of the Iron Age tribes again held sway. The Pictish kingdom, still perhaps a fairly loose confederation, now dominated the country north of the Forth and Clyde, with the exception of Argyll which was occupied by the

10 The Roman distance slab from Bridgeness at the east end of the Antonine Wall

11 The 'Traprain treasure': a hoard of Roman silverware from a native centre in south-east Scotland

kingdom of Dàl Riata. This latter group held strong Irish links (their leading dynasties identified Ulster as their place of origin), although they were probably descended for the most part from the indigenous peoples of Argyll. South of the Forth and Clyde were a series of small kingdoms, including the Gododdin, descendants of the Iron Age Votadini (later swallowed up by the expanding power of Northumbria, to the south), and the Britons of Strathclyde.

As in Roman times, the availability of some written records for the mid to late first millennium AD means that we are no longer dealing with a wholly prehistoric period. Nonetheless, most of the documentary evidence, with the exception of place-names, deals primarily with the activities of the political and social elite and tell us little about the lives of the majority of the population. These records can provide a broad outline of political developments, charting the gradual emergence of increasingly cohesive kingdoms, but integrating such information with the archaeological evidence is notoriously problematic.

Some of the archaeological evidence is remarkably similar to that of the Iron Age. Hillforts were refurbished or built anew, although they often took new forms. Some of the new hillforts contained strongly walled summits or citadels surrounded by walled terraces, giving a clear grading of space. Unlike their Iron Age antecedents these appear to have been monuments to the power of the lord or king more than symbols of communal strength.

While the homes of the social elite were often very visible in the landscape, the lower classes of society all but disappeared from view. No longer were the landscapes of the south and east full of stout timber houses of prosperous farmers. Although some houses of this period have been excavated in recent years, these lacked the monumentality of their Iron Age precursors and suggest that there was rather more differentiation in apparent wealth between the upper and lower ranks of society.

These distinctions are reflected too in the production of increasingly elaborate metalwork and bonework. A profusion of personal ornaments such as pins, brooches and combs, suggests that the nuances of personal appearance were becoming ever-greater factors in denoting social status in societies where there was a growing gulf between social classes.

Amongst the Picts a tradition evolved of erecting monumental carved stones, depicting animals, objects, people and, most commonly, abstract symbols (*12*). The purpose and meaning of these symbol stones have been the source of lengthy and vociferous debate between academic and amateur enthusiast alike. Yet most would agree that, whatever the specific meaning of this or that symbol, the stones were commissioned by the social elite to commemorate their own and their families' lives, deaths and achievements.

The adoption of Christianity by the various post-Roman peoples of Scotland, from around the fifth century AD onwards, marked an important break with the past. When Christianity became fully established among the Picts, some time

12 A Pictish symbol stone:
the rear view of the road-side
cross-slab at Aberlemno in
Angus (see Chapter 8)

after AD 700, the old symbols were still carved, but now mostly as adornments on Christian cross-slabs. The cultural influences and organisation of the early Church transcended the boundaries of the post-Roman tribes and states, drawing the people of what was soon to become Scotland into an increasingly cosmopolitan age. The associated spread of writing offered a new means by which rights and relationships could be formalised and recorded, and further distinguished the literate elite from the illiterate masses.

THE KINGDOM OF ALBA

By AD 1000, the post-Roman peoples had amalgamated, under the ascendant Scots of Dalriada, into the kingdom of Alba. All traces of an independent Pictish culture were by now extinguished, and lands south of the Forth and Clyde had been wrenched away from Northumbrian settlers. For the first time a nation existed which we can realistically claim as directly ancestral to modern Scotland. Despite the harrying of Vikings, who had settled the northern and western isles and parts of the north mainland, this enlarged kingdom continued to thrive and expand, as it crept into the light of a rather fuller written history.

2

Early settlers

The earliest inhabitants of Scotland, the wandering hunter-gatherers of the Mesolithic period and earlier, left few traces. The remains of their homes have almost all been wiped away by the natural forces of environmental change, and by the efforts of countless generations of their descendants who have transformed the land by cultivation, drainage and forest clearance. Rare survivals of Mesolithic settlement, such as the site of Kinloch on the Hebridean island of Rum, show that occupation was generally in fairly slight structures of timber or skins. Communities may have maintained semi-permanent base-camps, but most people would have spent much of their time on the move.

Until recently the settlement at Kinloch was the earliest known in Scotland, dating to around 7000 BC. A coastal settlement at Morton in Fife may be almost as early on the other side of the country. Mesolithic flints from high on the slopes of Ben Lawers, above Loch Tay in Perthshire, suggest that most areas and environmental niches were probably exploited to some extent even at this early date.

This accepted picture of rather slight and transitory Mesolithic dwellings has been shaken somewhat by the discovery in 2001 of a rather more substantial Mesolithic house at East Barns, near Dunbar in East Lothian. This oval, sunken-floored house measured nearly 7m across and had a roof supported by around 30 timber posts. Astoundingly, the initial radiocarbon dates suggested occupation perhaps as early as 7800-8300 BC, which would make East Barns the earliest known house in Scotland, although close in date to not dissimilar structures in Mount Sandel on the north coast of Ireland and Howick in north-east England.

With the adoption of farming, communities began to establish even more permanent settlements, although some degree of seasonal mobility may have

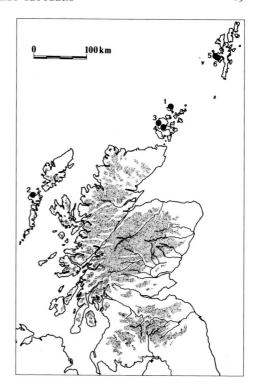

13 Map of sites in Chapter 2

remained part of the yearly round. The tending of arable plots tied people to their home base and probably helped create a new attitude to the relationship between communities and the land. Perhaps for the first time it became crucial to secure rights to particular parcels of land: claims could be established and maintained by constructing boundaries or enclosures, or by imprinting the land with permanent and substantial houses or monuments. Burial mounds could become particularly important, as they not only marked the presence of the community, but symbolised its ancestral links with the locality and thus its rights to live and farm the land.

   Early houses, however, remain elusive. As might be expected, they survive best where they were built of stone, rather than of perishable materials such as timber and turf (*13*). In the Neolithic period this tends to restrict survival to the far north and west, and particularly to the archipelagos of Orkney, Shetland and the Western Isles. Some of the settlements that survive in the north have few if any earthfast elements, and their counterparts in the lowlands will long since have been obliterated by the zealous arable cultivation of later generations. Very often, archaeological excavations in the lowlands recover small groups of shallow pits, and occasional hearths, containing sherds of Neolithic pottery or fragments of stone axes (*14*). It is not beyond the bounds of possibility that these are the sole, sad remnants of the lowland equivalents of Skara Brae.

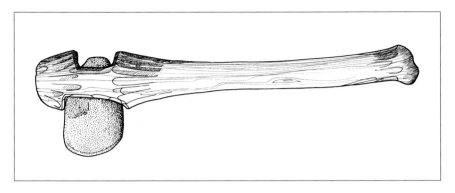

14 Stone axes were first used to clear land in virgin forest during the Neolithic period

Nonetheless, the few remarkable exceptions to the general scarcity of lowland Neolithic settlement can show quite different forms of settlement, the best example being the site of Balbridie in Aberdeenshire. This site was identified from air as a cropmark, that is a series of markings showing up usually in a ripening arable crop, caused by the presence of buried archaeological features such as ditches and post-holes (see pl. 44). When excavated in the late 1970s, a massive timber-framed building was revealed, with dimensions of around 24m by 10m (*15*), dating to around 3600 BC. This substantial structure seems to have been home to an early farming community who grew wheat and barley, and used pottery styles familiar from excavations in Orkney and elsewhere. The building was completely unlike any of the homesteads and villages discussed below; much more akin, in fact, to early farming settlements in France, Germany and the Netherlands.

For many years Balbridie stood as the sole exception to the apparent rule of small-scale, transitory Neolithic settlements in the south and east. Recently, however, the picture has changed. Excavations in 2001 at Claish Farm in Stirlingshire revealed the remains of a strikingly similar building, in this case rectangular with rounded end walls, and measuring around 25m long. Like Balbridie the structure at Claish was divided into several large rooms, and seems to have fulfilled a range of domestic and agricultural functions. Then in 2004, excavations at Crathes, just across the River Dee from Balbridie, revealed yet another massive timber building which seems to have burnt down between around 3950-3600 BC. These recent discoveries provide a salutary lesson that our best-surviving, and thus best-known sites, may present only a very limited perspective on Neolithic life.

KNAP OF HOWAR, PAPA WESTRAY, ORKNEY (1)
HISTORIC SCOTLAND
HY 483 518

How to get there

The small island of Papa Westray can be reached by ferry or plane from Kirkwall on
the mainland of Orkney (the site is just around 500m west of the airfield). Once there,
a short walk west down the sign-posted track from Holland farm takes you to Knap of
Howar, although the site itself is quite inconspicuous until you are almost upon it.

A Neolithic homestead

The remains of two rectangular buildings at Knap of Howar were first discovered
during the 1920s when gales and tides ripped away part of the coastline, exposing
the remains of buildings and midden spreads (*colour plate 1*). Excavations followed in
the 1930s, but little more than superficial sand and rubble were removed before the
site was taken into state care in 1937. Indeed, it was not until the 1970s that more
detailed excavations demonstrated that this was not only a pair of astonishingly
well-preserved Neolithic buildings, but, in fact, the oldest stone houses to be seen
anywhere in north-west Europe, dating to the period around 3500 – 3100 BC (*15*).

Knap of Howar is a good site from which to appreciate the massive landscape
changes that have occurred since the Neolithic period. Although the site now
lies on the edge of the beach, it seems that when it was originally occupied,
the houses lay in grassland behind the dunes. In fact, Papa Westray was probably

15 An artist's impression of the great timber hall at Balbridie, Aberdeenshire. The scale of the
structure can be gauged from the human figure at the entrance

linked at that time to the much larger island of Westray, now cut off by a shallow channel of just over a mile wide.

The site itself appears to have been a small farmstead of two conjoined rectangular buildings preserved up to around 1.6m, i.e. around head-height (16). A timber-framed roof of thatch or turf would originally have been supported partly by these walls and partly by posts, for which the post-holes were found during excavation. Both houses were dug partly into spreads of midden material, so there were clearly even older buildings on the site which have either not survived, or lie buried somewhere close to the excavated area.

Exploring the houses

The larger of the two preserved houses was entered through a timber door in its shorter, west end (the stone sill and jambs for the door can still be seen). The windowless interior would have been dark, but not too cramped. The first room to be entered had a low stone bench along one wall but few other surviving features. Beyond, through a timber partition, now marked by the line of upright slabs that helped support it, was an inner room with a hearth, wooden benches and a large stone quern, for grinding grain, embedded in the floor.

The excavator suggested that the inner room was a kitchen, for preparing and cooking food, while the outer might have been a more generalised living area. There are several other possibilities since many societies divide up their domestic space quite strictly. Perhaps the segregated areas related to activities associated with men and women, or perhaps the divisions were based on age or status.

A connecting door from the first house led into the second, smaller building. This, too, was divided into rooms, and had its own separate entrance from the outside. While it may have been a workshop of some kind, as the excavator suggested, it may well simply have been a second house, perhaps signifying that the extended family who lived at Knap of Howar was a little larger or more complex in its composition than might initially be imagined.

Fishers and farmers

From the numerous finds made during the excavations, Knap of Howar seems to have been home to a small, self-sufficient community. As we might expect in an area like Orkney, they made good use of all the resources available to them. Cattle, sheep and pigs were kept, and barley and wheat were cultivated. They also exploited wild animals, such as red deer, sea-birds, seals and whales, perhaps rather opportunistically. Fishing, predictably, played a large part in the economy, and some species, like cod, ling and large saithe, must have been caught by line-fishing from boats. Bone and stone tools denote a range of domestic crafts: tools in more perishable materials, such as wood, probably existed, but have long since decayed.

Although the overwhelming impression is of economic independence, the inhabitants of Knap of Howar nonetheless formed part of a much wider cultural

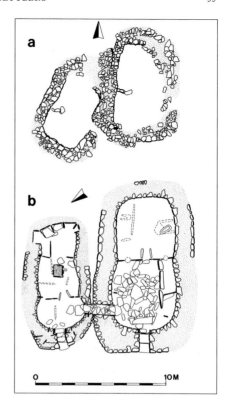

16 House plans from (a) Eilean Domhnuill
and (b) Knap of Howar

0   10M

group. Perhaps the main surviving expression of their cultural affiliations comes
in the form of their finely-made and highly decorated pottery, in a style known
as Unstan Ware (*18*), named after a chambered tomb in Orkney. The elegant
shallow, round-based bowls that dominate this pottery tradition not only link
the farmers of Knap of Howar to the people buried in the surrounding tombs
(see Chapter 3), but also show their much wider cultural links with other areas
in which similar pottery styles are found, such as in Aberdeenshire (for example,
the great timber building at Balbridie), and the Western Isles.

EILEAN DOMHNUILL, LOCH OLABHAT, NORTH UIST, WESTERN ISLES (2)
PRIVATE OWNERSHIP
NF 747 753

How to get there
Loch Olabhat lies in the north-west corner of North Uist, immediately north of
the A865 road which encircles the island. The islet known as Eilean Domhnuill
can be glimpsed from the road itself and can be reached by a ten minute walk

downhill across the peat bog. The stone causeway is passable in all but the most Hebridean of weather conditions.

The first crannog?

At around the same time as Knap of Howar was occupied in Orkney, a farming community of similar size constructed a largely man-made islet (or 'crannog') in Loch Olabhat in North Uist (*colour plate 2*); a site investigated by excavations in the late 1980s (*16*). Crannogs are a fairly common type of settlement in Scotland, but the vast majority seem to date much later, to the Iron Age or medieval periods. Radiocarbon dates show that this site was occupied by 3650 BC, if not earlier, and archaeological evidence suggests more or less continuous activity from then until around 2600 BC.

Over many generations a succession of turf-walled houses occupied the interior of the islet, protected from intruders by a timber fence or screen that was repeatedly modified and re-aligned (*17*). The houses themselves seem to have been taken down periodically, right to their foundations, and rebuilt on an adjacent spot.

Throughout the occupation, the islet was linked to the shore first by a timber gangway, and finally by a solid stone causeway. At various times the islet seems to have been submerged by rising water levels, only to be re-occupied when the waters receded. In the end, however, it disappeared beneath the surface of the loch altogether, not to re-appear for many centuries. It was this fortuitous occurrence (for archaeologists if not for the original inhabitants) that ensured its exceptional quality of survival.

In its final phase, the two conjoined, oblong, stone-footed structures that stood in the centre of the islet were strikingly similar to those at Knap of Howar. In addition, the huge quantities of pottery found at Eilean Domhnuill included many vessels and sherds of the characteristic Unstan Ware found at the Orcadian site (*18*). Nonetheless, there were clearly significant differences, not least of which was the immense effort put into the construction of the artificial islet of Eilean Domhnuill.

While there is little now to be seen of the Neolithic buildings, other than parts of two of the latest phase houses and the causeway (greatly rebuilt in recent years), it is still possible to appreciate the setting of the site and gain some feeling for the original settlement as it would once have been.

SKARA BRAE, ORKNEY (MAINLAND) (3)
HISTORIC SCOTLAND
HY 231 188

How to get there

Skara Brae lies on the Bay of Skaill, just over 6 miles (10km) north of Stromness along the B9056. It is well sign-posted, and reached by a short walk from the

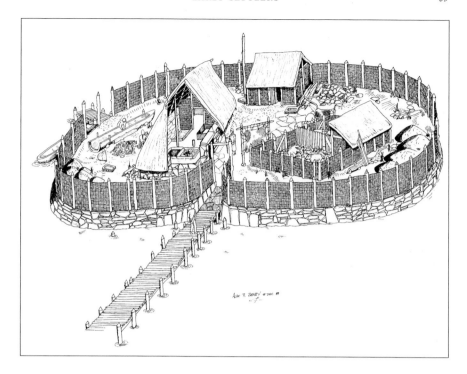

Above: 17 Eilean Domhnuill,
North Uist, reconstruction
drawing

Right: 18 Pottery from Eilean
Domhnuill; a. Unstan Ware,
and b. Hebridean Ware

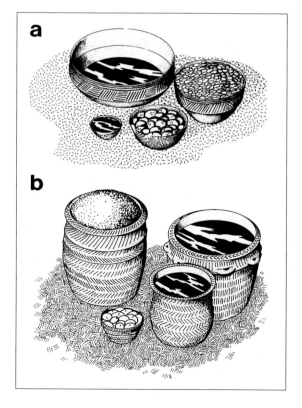

car park. There is a small visitor centre at the site which includes a display of some of the artefacts found during excavation and a reconstruction of one of the houses.

The village under the sand

While Knap of Howar boasts the oldest visible stone houses in north-west Europe, Skara Brae remains probably the most complex and best-preserved settlement of the Neolithic period (*colour plate 3*). First uncovered by a great storm around 1850, which tore away the dune face along part of the Bay of Skaill, the site comprises a near-complete village of clustered houses and interconnecting passages dating mostly to around 3000-2500 BC (*19*). Ten houses are visible today, but many more probably lie buried beneath the main complex, as this was a long-lived settlement that continuously evolved over many centuries.

The most striking features of the visible houses, which mostly represent the village as it was just before it was abandoned, are their extraordinary degree of preservation, and their apparent uniformity. The standard plan comprises a squarish room, some 6m by 6m internally, with a substantial central stone hearth. To each side of the hearth is a well-built box-bed, while across the hearth from the entrance is an imposing 'dresser'; a two-tier stone-shelved construction seemingly intended to display some unknown objects to anyone entering the

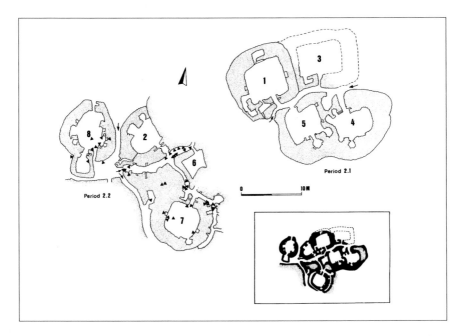

19 A simplified plan of Skara Brae, Orkney; the bottom right plan is a simplified view of the whole settlement. The more detailed segments show the earlier part (period 2.1) and the later additions (period 2.2) slightly 'pulled apart'

house. Such regularity of fixtures and fittings surely implies that strong social rules governed the laying out of houses, and it is a reasonable assumption that similar prescriptions dictated behaviour within them.

Most of the houses contain an assortment of stone-built shelves and cramped alcoves, and some give access to small cells with well-paved drains that appear to have been designed as lavatories. Several of the houses survive more or less to the their original wall height, from which they would originally have been capped by timber-framed roofs covered with thatch or turf.

There seems little doubt that the house interiors were meant to impress. To reach any of the houses, the visitor had to crouch and fumble their way through the low, narrow and tortuous passage that snaked through the sand to the doorway. This cramped trek, however, only served to accentuate the feeling of height and space once they could, finally, stand to full height in the hearth-lit interior. So much of the furniture of these houses was built in stone that, even today, we can glean a remarkable impression of what the Neolithic visitor would have seen. To what survives, however, we should add the long-vanished organic components, such as skin canopies over the box-beds, and perhaps richly decorated skins and furs on the walls and floors. What precious possessions might once have graced the stone dressers is now anyone's guess.

Life in the village

The architecture of Skara Brae seems to express a range of social relationships which appear rather contradictory to the modern eye. While the design of the houses seems to suggest that each was home to a small, self-contained family unit, the overall design of the settlement seems, by contrast, to reflect a tight-knit and interdependent community. While the main cluster of houses could only be entered from a common passage, and thus all shared a communal front door, each had its own timber door which could be barred from the inside, shutting off the rest of the village. The inhabitants of the sunken maze of dwellings seem to have had a deep sense of community and interdependence, yet maintained rigid divisions into separate family groups.

We know from the elaborate communal tombs of this period (see Chapter 3) that social identity and the ancestors were of central significance to Neolithic people. Skara Brae seems to reflect this same phenomenon, applied to daily life rather than death, for the houses and passages are dug down into middens, the detritus of earlier generations. The very act of building these houses would have thrown up all sorts of relics of the ancestors, fragments of decorated pottery, stone and bone tools. Stones carved with fine curvilinear designs along the passages, particularly concentrated at entrances and dividing points, provide a further link with the decoration seen in some of the more elaborate tombs. In a society where the ancestral dead were constantly revisited and venerated, the symbolism inherent in dwelling deep amid the debris of past lives must surely have been appreciated.

The layout of the village not only bound together the living community, but also gave a profound sense of shared ancestry and continuity with their forebears.

People apart?

The superficial uniformity of the houses may mask more subtle differences. House 8, for example, stood a little away from the main group, and lacked beds and a dresser. Was this perhaps a workshop of some kind, a communal meeting area, or the dwelling of a particular group of people? House 7 was part of the main group, but, unlike the others, could only be accessed by a winding side passage and was bolted shut from the outside rather than the inside. This house yielded more and stranger material than the others. A bull's skull lay on one bed, while dishes of red pigment, beads, pendants and other debris lay strewn around, and the bodies of two women had been buried beneath the floor. Was this perhaps a house with special religious significance, where people might reside at specific times apart from the larger group; perhaps a house for the ill or dying, for childbirth, for widows, or for worship, confinement or meditation? Interestingly, of the whole complex, Houses 7 and 8 were the only two to contain carved stones, again suggesting some special function or significance.

The wider world

The village at Skara Brae is rather later in date than the Knap of Howar farmstead and its inhabitants used a different kind of pottery, flat-based with elaborate incised or applied decoration. This pottery style, known as Grooved Ware is found across much of Britain, as far south as Wessex, and is associated with the great ritual monuments of the Neolithic (see Chapter 4) as well as being quite common on settlements of the period (*20*). Although they continued to farm and fish and meet most of their needs within the locality, as their ancestors had done for centuries, the inhabitants of Skara Brae seem to have had cultural affiliations that extended well beyond Orkney, and much further than those apparent in earlier Orcadian communities.

BARNHOUSE, ORKNEY (MAINLAND) (4)
LOCAL AUTHORITY OWNERSHIP
HY 308 126

How to get there

The settlement at Barnhouse forms part of a wider landscape of spectacular Neolithic monuments, including the nearby Stones of Stenness (see Chapter 4). Take the B9055 north from the Kirkwall-Stromness road and park at the Stones of Stenness (Historic Scotland) car-park. From there, a sign-posted path leads you to the partly rebuilt buildings by the shore of the Loch of Harray.

20 Grooved Ware

A second Skara Brae?

Barnhouse, the closest parallel for the remarkable settlement at Skara Brae was discovered and partly excavated only a few years ago, close to some of the best known ritual monuments of Orkney, including the tomb at Maes Howe (see Chapter 3), and the stone circles of Stenness and Brodgar (see Chapter 4). At Barnhouse, a settlement of at least 15 houses was found, dating slightly earlier than Skara Brae, from around 3100–2800 BC.

Although the design of the houses at Barnhouse is closely similar to those at Skara Brae, with central hearths, box-beds and dressers, there are some significant differences. The Barnhouse buildings were built above ground, rather than dug into a midden. Their turf-clad oval or oblong outside walls would have given few hints of their stone-faced, well-finished interiors. Although lacking the intimacy of inter-connecting entrance passages, a network of drains leading to common ditches show some thought for corporate life.

Bringing the house down

Like the buildings at Eilean Domhnuill in the Western Isles (see above) the Barnhouse buildings seem to have been repeatedly re-built on more or less the same site: one was re-built at least five times. The excavator has suggested that such events might have marked the death of the occupants, or at least of the head of the household.

Chiefs, priests or residents committees?

As at Skara Brae, there were two buildings that stood out from the rest, although in the case of Barnhouse, it could be demonstrated that one was clearly later than the other. The earlier, House 2, was effectively just a big house, twice the size of the others, better-built, and with more than its share of box-beds. The later house was a rather different construction: it was a more massive building, with fine stone walls, set on an artificial platform of clay and surrounded by a low wall. An elongated entrance passage aligned north-west, on the midsummer sunrise, gave access to a rather grand interior which, nonetheless, still contained the usual hearth and dresser.

The various theories put forward for the unusual buildings at Skara Brae apply equally to Barnhouse. The most obvious interpretation might see them as houses of successive chiefs, each outdoing his predecessor. Alternatively they may have been religious buildings or meeting places for groups derived from the various households that made up the village.

SCORD OF BROUSTER, SHETLAND (MAINLAND) (5)
PRIVATE OWNERSHIP
HU 255 516

How to get there
The houses and field systems of Scord of Brouster lie just west of Bridge of Walls along the A971, on rising ground above Brouster Farm. You can see some elements of the field systems from the road, but the complex extends over a considerable area and is best walked over.

A farming landscape
While Shetland lacks, so far, Neolithic houses to rival the preservation or complexity of Skara Brae, it makes up for this omission in the sheer quantity and extent of prehistoric houses and fields. These are particularly numerous in the west part of mainland, the best known being the partly excavated site of Scord of Brouster.

This site comprises several houses, clearance cairns, burial mounds, and irregular enclosures defined by meandering field walls. The whole complex occupies around 5 acres (2ha) of present-day moorland. Although long since abandoned to the advancing peat, this land was farmed for many centuries, from around 3200 BC to 1500 BC, and fields of barley must be imagined around the cairns and within the walled enclosures.

The earliest houses were of turf or timber and little has survived, but an excavated stone house, occupied between around 3000-2500 BC can be seen tagged onto the enclosure nearest the road. This house was only slightly smaller than its contemporaries at Skara Brae. The oval interior was dominated by a central hearth while the periphery was divided into six small cells by projecting piers of stone.

Although the settlement pattern of which it formed a part appears radically distinct from the clustered villages of Neolithic Orkney, the society it reflects

may not have been so very different. The landscape seems to have been carved
up and cleared for cultivation early on, whether by negotiation or diktat. The
houses were dispersed among their own fields and enclosures, emphasising the
independence of each family group, but, being in such close proximity, the
inhabitants must have co-operated in farming and other economic pursuits and
must have maintained a complex web of social contacts to settle rights to land
and resources.

STANYDALE, SHETLAND (MAINLAND) (6)
HISTORIC SCOTLAND
HU 285 502

How to get there
Follow the minor road south from the main Lerwick to Walls road (A971) west
of Bixter. Marker posts guide the way over the rough terrain from the road to
the site.

The temple on the moors
The extraordinary structure known engagingly as Stanydale Temple lies in a bleak
stretch of moorland on the west mainland of Shetland (*colour plate 4*). A scatter
of other houses, not unlike the excavated ones at nearby Scord of Brouster, lie
in the vicinity. You will pass an excavated and partially restored example as you
walk towards the main building. These houses, however, are dwarfed by the sheer
scale of Stanydale Temple.

Approaching the main building you are faced with a crescentic facade of
drystone walling pierced by a single entrance. This frontage stands to around
head-height, but the upper levels have been restored in recent decades. Sill
stones in the entrance passage mark the former position of two heavy timber
doors. Once through this passage the interior opens up into a large oval space,
some 13m long by 7m, with various stone-walled recesses set around the inner
end. In the centre are two great post-holes which once held the ridge-posts of a
truly massive timber-framed roof that would have stood well over 6m above the
floor. For the Neolithic farmers used to the cramped confines of their own small
homes among the fields, this would doubtless have been an awe-inspiring sight.

Overseas aid
Fragments of spruce found when the site was excavated show that the builders
made use of driftwood (in this case from North America) to furnish them with
timbers of appropriate size for the roof supports. Clearly, in an area never blessed
with great forest cover, the massive timbers of the Stanydale roof would have
been a significant statement of command over scarce resources.

Pagan church or chieftain's hall?

The purpose of the Stanydale building remains a mystery, and the early excavations on the site were of little help in this regard. The roofing requirements and size of the building suggest that it would have been built as a communal enterprise. It may have been the home of a local chief, or perhaps a gathering place for the community. Numerous small hearths around the periphery suggest that it did not function as a large single-family house which might have been expected to yield a large central hearth.

Its use may have been based around ritual, or more prosaically it might have functioned as a form of village hall for the dispersed households scattered around the moors. Either way, it is tempting to suggest that Stanydale, like the larger buildings at Barnhouse and Skara Brae, signalled the emergence of special buildings with a function quite distinct from the undifferentiated farming settlements of earlier periods.

3

Tombs of the first farmers

The few early settlements which have been excavated in Scotland are overwhelmingly outnumbered by the profusion of Neolithic burial mounds. The houses of the dead seem everywhere much more visible than those of the living. This is not purely a Scottish phenomenon. In fact, throughout much of Europe the scale and permanence of Neolithic tombs is in marked contrast to the transient nature of contemporary houses, which were often lightly built of timber or turf.

The chambered tombs of Scotland represent just one regional manifestation of a burial tradition that permeated the whole of north-west Europe between around 4000 and 2000 BC. These megalithic ('big stone') monuments each comprise an inner room, or burial chamber, usually reached by a passage, set within a stone cairn.

From this basic principle sprang a wealth of variant designs. Yet in all cases, the building of such a tomb required an extraordinary endeavour on the part of the local community. Stones had to be gathered or quarried, moved to the desired location, and set into place. Some were enormous slabs (the eponymous megaliths) which were favoured particularly for the walls of the burial chambers, and for imposing façades. Such projects must have diverted significant amounts of labour from the more mundane activities of farming, fishing and the gathering of food.

The sites described in this chapter come mostly from the north and west of the country, and particularly from Orkney, where the native flagstones are ideal as a drystone building material (21). Similar monuments, however, were built in the south and east, although the timber, turf and earth commonly used for construction survives less well in the archaeological record. The excavation in

21 Map of sites in Chapter 3

1997, however, of an earthen burial mound at Fordhouse, on the National Trust for
Scotland's property at House of Dun, Montrose, revealed an early stone chamber
and passage deeply buried in the body of a Bronze Age mound. More such surprises
undoubtedly await discovery in parts of Scotland where the combination of building
materials and later disturbance have been less kind than they have in Orkney.

BARPA LANGASS, NORTH UIST, WESTERN ISLES (7)
PRIVATE OWNERSHIP
NF 838 657

How to get there

Barpa Langass is a visible as a great mound of stone on the skyline from miles
around. It lies in the heart of North Uist and is reached from the A867 just by
the turn off for the B894. A muddy trail leads the short distance uphill to the
tomb from the road. Take a torch if you want to enter the chamber.

Changing lands

Barpa Langass sits high on a bleak hillside over-looking mile upon mile of barren
peatlands (*22*). Yet, when this great tomb was first built, over 5000 years ago, it

22 Barpa Langass

would have dominated a wholly different landscape. The peat, which now chokes the interior of North Uist, was yet to form, held in check by a warmer, drier climate. Instead the land would have been dotted with patches of scrub woodland, pasture, and the settlements and fields of the Neolithic tomb builders.

The great cairn

At 5m high and 25m across, Barpa Langass is an impressive pile of stone, even if little of its structure is visible from the outside. Originally it probably had a more regular appearance than it does now. There would have been a kerb of large boulders demarcating the bottom of the cairn, and possibly well-built outer walls, giving it the appearance of a huge stone drum (*23*). Five thousand years of stone-robbing, however, mean that we can never be sure quite how it was meant to look.

The crouched passage

Even today it is possible to squeeze along the narrow passage into the simple, oval burial chamber, which survives completely intact. It is quite an experience to peer around the boulder-clogged interior by torchlight (even more so if others are clattering around on the cairn above). However, entry to the chamber is not to be recommended for the claustrophobic.

Space and society

Clearly this was a place where only a few could have access, and which had to be entered in single file. It may be significant that the entrance led off a forecourt, where a larger group could assemble. There appear to be clues in the very architecture of the tomb which suggests that some basic hierarchical principles operated in the society that built and used these monuments.

23 Barpa Langass, artist's reconstruction

CAMSTER, CAITHNESS (8)
HISTORIC SCOTLAND
ND 260 441

How to get there
The two large Camster cairns lie around 5 miles (8km) north of West Clyth, sign-posted from the A9. For once, a torch is unnecessary as the chambers have been restored and fitted with lights.

Ancient mounds
The Grey Cairns of Camster are among the earliest stone monuments in Scotland, seemingly dating to around 3500 BC, around the time of the great timber hall at Balbridie and the small farming settlement at Knap of Howar (see Chapter 2). They are also among the best preserved funerary monuments of the Neolithic period in Britain (*colour plate 5*). Their massive scale and moorland location have presumably saved them from the ravages of later agriculture that have destroyed the majority of tombs elsewhere.

The round cairn
Like Barpa Langass, the smaller of the Camster cairns takes the form of a huge circular mound of stone (*24*). At about 4m high and 18m in diameter, it is a little smaller than Barpa Langass, but unlike the Hebridean tomb, the Camster round cairn has been thoroughly excavated and cleared of rubble, giving a rather better idea of how the interior was meant to appear.

24 The round cairn at Camster, Caithness, during excavation of the forecourt

On entering, the visitor has to bow and almost crawl along the constricted passage; as at Skara Brae you must earn entry. Once in the chamber, however, the space opens out letting you stand to full height and take in the striking masonry and corbelled roof. Unlike the modest single chamber at Barpa Langass, pairs of large upright slabs divide the chamber at Camster into three distinct compartments. These so-called 'tripartite' chambers are a distinctive early form in the north of Scotland, and, as we shall see, seem to be ancestral to the later, more complex chamber forms.

The long cairn

Close by lies the second Camster cairn, a massive elongated mound of stone, nearly 70m long, by 20m across. The scale of this construction gives some idea of the extraordinary efforts that Neolithic farmers, in a fairly marginal part of Caithness, were able to devote to the veneration of their dead. Along the edges, well-built walls hold back the jumble of rubble which form the body of the cairn. At both ends, stone 'hornworks' project from the mound to form imposing facades and define forecourts. The north-east forecourt is the wider of the two, and gives the appearance of being the business end. It is here that the architecture of the tomb seems to focus the visitor's attention.

The life of the tomb

Despite its appearance, the long cairn began life as two separate small round cairns, not unlike the one described above. Each had its own chamber, one simple and one 'tripartite', now reached via passages entered from the side of the long cairn. Yet, shortly after these discrete monuments were erected, they were both enveloped in the huge body of stonework which was to form the long cairn.

This event seems to represent a major change of mind on the part of the tomb builders. Instead of two monuments, there was now just one; instead of round cairns, there was a long, horned mound; instead of south-east facing entrance passages, there was now a north-east facing forecourt, with no corresponding entrance; and instead of two fairly modest heaps of stone, there was now a single gigantic edifice.

Internal lines of walling suggest that the long cairn itself may have been built in several stages, perhaps over a number of years, or even generations. Perhaps over this time, fashions and beliefs evolved and changed, and tombs appropriate for earlier generations seemed too modest, or otherwise inappropriate to their descendants.

Spoils of the tombs

It is an unfortunate but inevitable fact of archaeological life that the best preserved and most obvious monuments in the landscape tended to be set upon by zealous antiquarians and their shovels, long before the principles of modern excavation and the battery of accompanying scientific techniques had developed. As a result, we often know very little about the archaeological deposits within some of the most impressive monuments. Camster is no exception, as the tombs were emptied during the nineteenth century with very little attention to detailed recording. Some skeletons, pottery and flints were found, but a fuller understanding of how these monuments were used to house the Neolithic dead had to wait several more generations of archaeological development.

CAPO, ABERDEENSHIRE (9)
FORESTRY COMMISSION
NO 633 664

How to get there
The long barrow (or mound) at Capo lies within a fenced clearing within a conifer plantation. Take the sign-posted minor road about 5 miles(8km) south of Laurencekirk on the A94. A sign-posted path leads to the site from the parking area.

Earthen mounds
The stone cairns of the north and west are generally the most obvious Neolithic tombs in the landscape today. Further south and east, however, many earthen mounds containing Neolithic burials survive within the modern agricultural landscape; often as tree-covered islands in arable fields where they have proved too cumbersome to cultivate and too large to remove.

A southern cousin?

The Capo long barrow has dimensions almost identical to those of the Camster long cairn; but built of turf and earth rather than stone. The wider, east end probably covers earlier burials and timber structures; much as the Camster cairn encompasses earlier tombs. The two monuments probably relate to the same burial tradition and date to the same broad period. Without excavation, however, it is impossible to be sure.

PITNACREE, PERTHSHIRE (10)
PRIVATE OWNERSHIP
NN 929 554

How to get there

Take the A827 from Ballinluig heading for Aberfeldy. After about 2½ miles (4km) you will see this distinctive tree-covered circular mound in an arable field just by the road on the left (if you reach the bridge over the Tay you have gone too far). It is best observed from the road.

A story from the earth

Like Capo (see above) the Pitnacree mound belongs to the southern and eastern Scottish series of earthen monuments that get rather less attention than their better-preserved stone counterparts in the north and west. Nonetheless, when Pitnacree was excavated in the 1960s an extraordinary sequence of burial and ritual was uncovered.

Around 3500 BC a mortuary house seems to have been set up, formed around two huge posts, each 1m in diameter and probably about 3-4m high. Later, a horseshoe-shaped earthen enclosure, revetted with stone, was built. This was associated with cremation burials and was very probably an earthen version of a chambered tomb, not unlike Barpa Langass in size and shape. Later again, the whole construction was augmented, sealing all the earlier structures and burials under one huge round mound (25).

ISBISTER, SOUTH RONALDSAY, ORKNEY (11)
LOCAL AUTHORITY
ND 470 845

How to get there

The road to Liddle Farm is sign-posted from the B9041 at the southern end of South Ronaldsay (attached by causeway to mainland Orkney). There is a small display area at the farm and guides will take you from there to the tomb. The roof that now covers the chamber is a modern addition.

25 The tree-covered mound of Pitnacree, Perthshire, prior to excavation

A sealed chamber

The tomb at Isbister, perched near the edge of the impressive sea-cliffs at the south of South Ronaldsay, appeared before excavation as a fairly unimpressive mound, and thus escaped the attentions of nnieteenth-century excavators. When it was excavated, in the 1970s, it was found that the tomb had been sealed during the Neolithic period with midden and stones. Below this mass of debris, the remains of the last people to be buried in the tomb, remained strewn around the floor of the chamber.

The chamber is rather more elaborate than those at Camster, around 8m long with five compartments, some fitted with high shelves, and a series of small side cells (26). These cells were only about 1m high, and were presumably intended to receive burials or offerings. When found, they contained heaps of human skulls. More piles of bones, usually with a skull (although not all coming from the same individual) lay at intervals along the sides of the main chamber. Also present were fragments of fine Unstan pottery, like that from the Knap of Howar (see Chapter 2). From the available radiocarbon dates it seems that the tomb was built perhaps a couple of centuries before 3000 BC and used for several centuries thereafter.

Neolithic people

The remains of around 340 people were found within the Isbister tomb, although many of the skeletons were incomplete, and some were represented by only a few bones. These people represented a cross-section of the Neolithic community. Men, women and children of all ages were present, with the exception only of new-born babies.

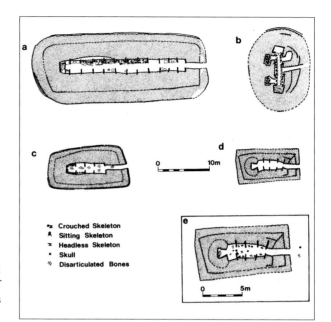

26 Chambered tombs in Orkney; this collection of plans comprises (a) Midhowe (b) Isbister (c) Yarso (d) and (e) Holm of Papa Westray South. It shows the distribution of human remains and finds within the chambers

Detailed study of the Isbister bones reveals a great deal about the people of Neolithic Orkney. Average heights for men worked out at around 5ft 7in (1.70m), while women averaged 5ft 4in (1.63m): not so very different from modern populations. The whole population seems to have been muscular and well-used to heavy physical work (about half of the adults had degenerative disease of the spine resulting from heavy labour). Although injuries involving broken bones were common, there was no sign of deliberately inflicted injuries. The skulls of many women bore marks caused by carrying loads by means of a 'brow-band'; signs presumably of some formal division of labour between the sexes.

Life expectancy was low by modern standards, and even those who survived childhood could not be overly optimistic about reaching thirty. Hardly anyone reached fifty, and those who did were almost exclusively male. The rigours of childbirth presumably shortened the life expectancy of women.

Grim as it seems, such a population structure is not uncommon among pre-industrial societies. Even our ancestors of a couple of centuries ago would have faced similar conditions. The effects on the Neolithic community, however, would have been striking. The population as a whole would have seemed very young. Old age would have been so rare that the old may well have had a special, perhaps venerated status. Extended rather than nuclear family households would have been more or less dictated by the population structure, to allow for enough able-bodied adults to maintain the community.

Tombs such as Isbister were clearly not the preserve of a 'leisure class' of nobility or priests. They seem to imply egalitarian communities whose members could all anticipate respect in death and look forward to taking their place in the tomb they helped build and maintain. There undoubtedly were organisers, perhaps priests or elders, who co-ordinated the labour of the group and presumably officiated in the building process and conduct of rituals. Yet there is nothing among the bones to suggest that such individuals were other than farmers and fishers who shared in the labour they directed and merged with their neighbours in death into the faceless community of ancestors.

Clan of the eagles?

Of the many animal and bird bones sealed into the tomb, the most unusual were the large numbers of sea eagles, and deposits of talons. Indeed the remains of eagle were so numerous that it has been suggested that the bird may have been a totem or clan badge for the community. This intriguing deposit has a close parallel at Cuween, another Orcadian tomb, where 24 dog skulls had been placed in the chamber. Perhaps then the people of Neolithic Orkney inhabited a developed tribal society where various groups venerated or identified themselves with particular animals or birds. If so, it is not hard to see how the sea eagle, a majestic white-tailed bird with a wing-span of over 2m, would have appealed.

MIDHOWE, ROUSAY, ORKNEY (12)
HISTORIC SCOTLAND
HY 372 304

How to get there

Midhowe lies on the island of Rousay off mainland Orkney. Once you reach the island by ferry from mainland Orkney, head north-west along the B9064 for about 5 miles (8km), then follow the signs along the footpath down to the coast. The chambered tomb lies just south of the broch of Midhowe (see Chapter 6), preserved in its open-top excavated state inside what appears as a miniature aircraft hangar. An ingenious system of gangways supported by scaffolding allows the visitor to look down into the tomb and shows its layout and scale to good effect.

Island of the dead?

Rousay is remarkable for its density of surviving chambered tombs. Fifteen tombs in all are known on this small island, several of them quite massive in scale (four of them are in state care). Each tomb seems to occupy a discrete pocket of land, suggesting that each may have belonged to a single small community, perhaps acting as a territorial marker. The number of tombs and their distribution in the landscape seems strikingly similar to that of farms in the early modern period.

The lengthening tomb

The outer cairn at Midhowe was similar in size to the long cairn at Camster (*colour plate 6*). Again like Camster, the cairn was no jumble of stones, but had a carefully walled exterior surviving to well over head-height. At Midhowe this had been taken a stage further, with stones arranged at angles to create a decorative 'herring-bone' effect along the east face. Unlike Camster, however, the elaborate exterior concealed an equally elaborate interior.

The chambers inside the early Orcadian cairns were simple constructions divided into two or three stalls. Later, however, these bi- and tripartite chambers were superseded by elaborated and enlarged variations on the same basic theme. The builders of Midhowe took the basic concept of the tripartite interior, but stretched it out to encompass twelve separate compartments with one long corridor, 23m long, leading through them.

As you pass through the tomb, the first few simple compartments give way to compartments with low benches built into their east walls. Finally, the twelfth compartment is divided into two by low slabs, with a paved inner area. It is difficult now to imagine the impact on the senses that this journey would have had in Neolithic times; walking, crouched, along the cramped and airless passage lit only by flickering torches, under the gaze of the fleshless skulls and dessicated corpses of the ancestors.

The community of ancestors

Chambered tombs were not simple burial vaults for the periodic disposal of the community's dead. Instead, the remains of individuals were often mixed-up and rearranged into groups, perhaps of skulls or long bones, as if to subsume the identity of the deceased individual within the community of ancestors (*26*).

At Midhowe, nine corpses were laid out along the side benches that flanked the stalls, crouched on their sides and facing into the main corridor with their backs to the wall. The skulls from three of those bodies had been removed and placed upright on the bench. As well as these fairly complete skeletons, the partial remains of at least another fifteen people were found in the tomb in various combinations, piled in the compartments or stowed under the benches. In some cases only the skull was present.

Revisiting the dead

The burials from Midhowe and elsewhere, so alien to modern western traditions, show that burial in the Neolithic was no once-and-for-all process. Seemingly the chambered tomb was regarded as a house of the dead, where the ancestors lived in a dark, dank, silent counterpart to the warm, bustling homes of the living. There, they could be visited, perhaps at particular festivals or important ritual occasions in the life of the community. Certainly the physical remains of the dead were at various times removed, replaced, mixed up and re-ordered, suggesting that they played a part in the rituals of daily life. Offerings of food or drink and fine pottery vessels were also made within the tomb, perhaps to appease the ancestors, or to support requests for favours or blessings.

Freeing the spirits

The over-representation of larger bones, such as skulls and long bones, suggests that bodies sometimes arrived at the tomb with the flesh already gone, probably after a period of exposure of the corpse. Such rites, usually seen as a form of ritual purification, letting the spirit escape from the decaying remains of the body, persisted in some Native American communities until quite recently.

Nonetheless, the crouched burials laid out on the benches at Midhowe must represent entire corpses laid to rest within the tomb itself. It may be that these burials represent the last group of burials put into the tomb, while their predecessors had been pushed aside and gathered up to form the piles of disarticulated bones found around the complete bodies. The removal of the heads of some of the crouched burials may have been the start of this process of dismantling the decaying bodies. If this is the case, then an even later stage in the process must have been the removal of bones from the chamber, as the bone heaps did not contain all the bones that should otherwise have littered the chamber floor.

MAES HOWE, ORKNEY (MAINLAND) (13)
HISTORIC SCOTLAND
HY 318 127

How to get there

The great green mound that covers Maes Howe is clearly visible and sign-posted, close to the right hand side of the A965 from Kirkwall to Stromness on mainland Orkney. Although built and used in the Neolithic period, the tomb was re-used in Viking times (see Chapter 9). It forms part of a complex of ritual monuments in this part of Orkney, including the henges of Brodgar and Stenness (see Chapter 4).

The encircled tomb

Dating to around 3000 BC, Maes Howe is, by some distance, the most accomplished chambered tomb in Britain. Although the outer part of the entrance passage has been restored, and the topmost capping of the chamber roof is modern, a visit to Maes Howe gives an excellent impression of how the tomb would have appeared in its heyday. Before reaching the mound itself you must first pass through the large enclosure that surrounds it, its low grassy bank encircling a shallow inner ditch (27). Crossing the causeway you see the full scale of the tomb, some 7m high and 35m across towering above the interior of the enclosure and set on a levelled platform of clay and stone; the same materials that form the body of the mound. When not in use, the passage into the mound would have been solidly blocked by a large boulder which sites in a niche to the left of the entrance (alternatively the stone may have given privacy to those conducting rituals within the chamber). Opening and closing the tomb would have been an effort in itself; the prelude to rituals of burial and worship.

Once in the passage, as ever, you must bow your head as you walk towards the chamber (*28*). Some of the stones lining the sides of the passage are enormous slabs that would have taken a huge effort to manoeuvre into place. These give a strikingly smooth texture to the walls and their sheer monumentality gives forewarning of what is to come in the chamber itself.

The soaring chamber

The chamber is almost square with sides about 4.5m long (*colour plate 7*). The walls rise vertically almost to shoulder height then begin to converge as they rise. The roof is an extraordinary piece of architecture, soaring upwards as high as the chamber is broad with a fine corbelled roof. At each corner, stone buttresses help support the roof, each faced with a massive orthostat or standing stone which serves to accentuate the impression of height. By any standards this structure was an outstanding achievement of prehistoric construction, an intricate balance of art and architecture with few rivals anywhere in prehistoric Europe.

Leading off from the chamber are three small side cells or recesses, set at about waist-height. These finely built stone boxes would presumably have received burials, and were probably once sealed with stone blocks which now rest on

27 An early view of Maes Howe, Orkney, by James Farrer, first published in 1862

28 Looking out along the passage at Maes Howe, Orkney

the chamber floor. Their size might suggest that each was intended for just a single occupant. Unfortunately the tomb has long since been cleared out of any burial deposits. When the antiquarian James Farrer opened the mound in 1861 it became clear that many other visitors had come and gone in the centuries before him, leaving nothing of the Neolithic tomb contents (see Chapter 9).

Conceptual change
Maes Howe, as well as being unusually grand, represents a wholly different type of tomb design from Midhowe. While Midhowe and other 'stalled ' cairns were based around long chambers divided into numerous compartments, tombs of Maes Howe type focused on a single large squarish chamber, giving access to a number of small recesses or cells. The use of space within the tomb was thus quite different and presumably so too were the rituals carried out inside.

The living and the dead
From the pottery found within them it is possible to link some of the tomb types found in Orkney to the settlements of the same period. Thus the tripartite and 'stalled' cairns, like Midhowe, contain Unstan pottery very similar to that found at settlements like Knap of Howar (see Chapter 2). By contrast, tombs of Maes Howe type contain Grooved Ware like that found at Skara Brae and Barnhouse. Although

the styles overlap in date, Grooved Ware seems to have appeared rather later. It also has a much wider distribution, being found on sites of similar type as far away as Wessex, where it is found on henge monuments like Stonehenge and Avebury.

Maes Howe lies so close to the settlement of Barnhouse, that it seems more than likely that the inhabitants of that settlement would have witnessed the rites carried out at the tomb. Perhaps they also helped built it, and perhaps some were even buried within it.

Tribal Orkney?

One of the most intriguing questions relating to the Neolithic in Orkney is the relationship between the users of Unstan Ware, who lived in small settlements like Knap of Howar and buried their dead in stalled tombs like Midhowe; and the users of Grooved Ware who occupied villages like Skara Brae and Barnhouse, and buried their dead in increasingly monumental tombs like Maes Howe. The apparent chronological overlap suggests that the difference wasn't simply down to one set of cultural values replacing the other. Perhaps there were ethnic, tribal or religious distinctions. Or perhaps the users of Grooved Ware represented an emerging elite within society that became increasingly dominant.

The coming of chiefs

It has been calculated that Maes Howe would have taken around 40,000 man-hours to build. That is around four times the effort that went into the communal tomb at Isbister, and about eight times the labour expended on many smaller Orcadian tombs. Yet, despite the greater labour that was devoted to their construction, tombs like Maes Howe seem in general to have housed fewer bodies than earlier tombs. And there were fewer of them; only some ten are known, as against around 50 'stalled' cairns. So, more people laboured for longer, apparently for the benefit of a smaller number. Perhaps in Maes Howe we can see the emergence of more overt social hierarchies where certain people were able to command and control the labour of others, and where the tombs that once housed the community of ancestors were now reserved for the privileged elite.

The winter chamber

Maes Howe is one of many Neolithic monuments which incorporates astronomic alignments within its design (we will see more examples in Chapter 4). The long entrance passage at Maes Howe points to the south west, in the direction of the midwinter sunset. Thus, on the shortest day of the year, as the sun dies, beams of red sunlight illuminate the passage and throw their light onto the back wall of the chamber. Such a dramatic effect on such a significant day can surely be no coincidence. It must surely mean that rituals involving the bones of the ancestors were played out in the chamber on the shortest day of the year; presumably rituals connected with the death of the old year and the birth of new. Maes

Howe, thus, formed a conceptual opposite to houses of the living aligned on the midsummer sunrise, like Structure 8 at nearby Barnhouse (see Chapter 2).

DWARFIE STANE, HOY, ORKNEY (14)
HISTORIC SCOTLAND
HY 244 005

How to get there
The Dwarfie Stane lies on the Orcadian island of Hoy reached by ferry from Stromness on mainland Orkney. Disembarking at Mo Ness you take the B9049 south for 1¼ miles (2km) then head south on the minor road to Rackwick for a further 1¼ miles (2km). The tomb lies in a wind-blasted valley at the foot of Ward Hill, the highest hill in Orkney and is both visible and sign-posted on the south side of the road.

The rock-cut tomb
The Dwarfie Stane is one of the least conventional of all chambered tombs. Although empty of burial deposits, and effectively undatable, it is assumed to be Neolithic on the basis of its form and design. Rather than a built chamber, this tomb has been formed by hollowing out a massive block of red sandstone where it was found (29). The stone presents a striking landmark, visible from some distance around. Up close, the stone seems huge, measuring 8.5 by 4m, by about 2m high, with red veins of haematite marking out its north end. Inside is a short passage giving access to two small side cells. At the entrance lies a massive block of stone presumably used to block the access.

Early visitors
Unsurprisingly the lonely situation of the Dwarfie Stane and its mysterious character attracted those of a romantic disposition from at least the eighteenth century, as a series of graffiti inscriptions shows. Perhaps the most intriguing is an inscription carved in Persian lettering reading 'I have sat two nights and so learnt patience'. Beside it is the name Major W Mounsey spelt backwards in Latin and dated 1850. Mounsey was apparently a British spy active in and around Persia at the time.

CAIRNHOLY, DUMFRIES AND GALLOWAY (15)
HISTORIC SCOTLAND
NX 518 540

How to get there
The two Cairnholy chambered tombs are set about 150m apart on a hillside overlooking Wigtown Bay; an impressive and commanding spot. The minor road

29 The Dwarfie Stane, Hoy, Orkney

to the site is sign-posted from the main road around 3¾ miles (6km) south-east of Creetown.

Away from the isles

Although the chambered tombs of Orkney rather overwhelm those of the rest of the country, comparable monuments were built right across Scotland, particularly down the west coast, and beyond to Ireland, and the Atlantic coasts of Europe. The two neighbouring tombs at Cairnholy, excavated in 1949, are amongst the best preserved in the south-west.

Litter from the feast

The southern is the more impressive, partly for its great size, which compares with many of the larger Orkney tombs, but more particularly for its fine crescent-shaped facade of massive close-set standing stones. This imposing edifice is out of all proportion to the small, simple chamber, and suggests that gatherings here concentrated outside the tomb, in the forecourt, rather than in the cramped confines of the chamber. This impression was confirmed by excavation which showed the presence of a hearth and a post-hole in the forecourt, which had been sealed under a layer of stones when the tomb was finally closed. Broken pottery fragments also littered the forecourt, perhaps the debris of ritual or funerary feasts. The many finds suggest that the tomb was used for burial many centuries after its construction, perhaps as late as 2000 BC.

The portal stone

The northern cairn has been badly robbed of stone over the centuries, and is only half the size of its neighbour, but the inner of the two compartments in the chamber is still roofed. A massive standing stone, some 3m tall, marks the entrance, suggesting that here too, the visual impact of the monument was meant to be striking.

BALNAURAN OF CLAVA, HIGHLAND (16)
HISTORIC SCOTLAND
NH 752 439

How to get there

Drive east from Inverness along the B9006 until just past the Culloden Visitor Centre. Take the minor road south, following the signs to the car-park by the wooded enclosure in which the cairns now lie.

Tombs and standing stones

Many Scottish burial mounds incorporate massive standing stones, whether forming a facade as at Cairnholy, or supporting the chamber as at Maes Howe. In the area around modern-day Inverness, however, a regional tradition seems to have evolved in which tombs and circles of standing stones were used as distinct elements to create a new type of burial monument. These are known as Clava cairns, after the cemetery at Balnauran of Clava.

The linear cemetery

While chambered cairns in Orkney and elsewhere usually occur as isolated monuments, or less commonly in pairs, the individuals monuments at Balnauran of Clava form a small cemetery. This may be at least in part because they were no longer intended for constant re-use by successive generations. At Clava it seems that a new death may have necessitated a new tomb.

Encircled tombs

These tombs are generally round with well-defined kerbs of large boulders, and their chambers are simple and undivided. They are also usually rather smaller than the largest of the Orkney tombs. Their key distinguishing feature, however, is that each is surrounded by a ring of standing stones.

Sun-gazers

The three largest tombs monuments lie close together in a line running north-east to south-west (30). At either end are chambered tombs, with passages aligned, as at Maes Howe, on the midwinter sunset to the south-west. This alignment is reflected in the surrounding standing stones, which are graded in height so that the largest also lie to the south-west. When the tombs were built the area would probably have been clear of trees, making visible the movement of the pale midwinter sun on the horizon.

The closed tomb

The third large tomb, set between the other two, has no entrance or passage but instead is formed of a solid ring of stones with an open central area. Like its neighbours, however, this ring cairn has an outer ring of standing stones.

Last rites?

The tombs at Clava had been cleared out of their burials and other deposits many years ago, although some cremated human remains were found within the chamber of the ring cairn during the 1950s. Nonetheless, recent excavations have shed some light on their development and provided some dating evidence. It appears that the first of them may have been built as late as 2000 BC, one of the last flourishes of the tradition that began with the chambered tombs and related structures. The ring cairn may be even later.

Lost symbols

The Clava cairns were clearly built to precise specifications, incorporating elements which are difficult to explain in functional terms. Several of the stones built into the cairns, for example, display 'cup-and-ring marks'; rounded depressions and circles laboriously pecked into the stone. The cairn nearest to the

30 Balnauran of Clava, Highland

car park has a particularly fine cup-marked rock built into its kerb, and another towards the inner end of its passage. In several cases these were clearly made before the stones were built into the cairn and may derive from earlier graves or monuments (see, for example, Ballochmyle in Chapter 4).

The cairns were also carefully kerbed with large boulders, graded in size (like the stones of the surrounding circle) to highlight the importance of the south-west sector. The south-west of the cairn, and the parts of the chamber facing the entrance had a preponderance of reddish stones, perhaps to reflect and accentuate the warm glow of the setting midwinter sun: by contrast, the north-easterly facing parts had whiter stones. From the platform around the ring cairn run several stone 'rays' or low causeways, which join the platform to the outer circle of stones. All of these separate elements appear to have been constructed as one operation, and indicate a complex design, rather than a series of ad hoc additions.

Ancestor's house or chieftain's grave?

Where Clava-type tombs have produced evidence of burial it appears that only one or two bodies were buried within them, and the lack of access to the ring cairns seems to suggest that there was no intention here of revisiting the physical remains of the dead once they had been buried. There is little to suggest, then, that these were the communal tombs of local farmers, periodically re-stocked with the dead of the locality. Like Maes Howe in Orkney, these highly formalised and labour-intensive constructions, built in tune with the movements of the heavens, seem designed to receive only the privileged few; perhaps successive members of powerful lineage or dynasty.

4

Sacred places

By the time of the later chambered tombs, in the centuries after 3000 BC, monuments built solely for the dead were receding in importance. Instead, the dominant monuments of the later part of the Neolithic, from around 2900–2000 BC, were large ritual centres, often incorporating complex arrangements of timber posts and standing stones (*31*). The scale of these new monuments far exceeded even the largest tombs.

Almost all parts of the country seem to have witnessed the appearance of these centres, sometimes springing from earlier, less formal places of burial or worship. The phenomenon is so widespread, in fact, that it must surely signal the emergence of new and more powerful rulers, able to marshal labour on a scale not previously witnessed.

Many of these new monuments took the form of henges; large circular enclosures surrounded by a ditch with an external bank. This is the opposite of what you might expect of defensive enclosures, where the ditch would lie outside the bank to hinder attackers. Henges were clearly designed for an altogether different purpose; as if to keep something in rather than keep something out. As before, Orkney seems to have been a key centre for new developments in this period. Indeed, although henges take their name from Stonehenge in Wessex, it is in Scotland that the earliest examples appeared.

Elsewhere, even where no traces survive above ground, these ritual sites can still be found as cropmarks preserved under ploughed fields. Indeed the majority are known only through the evidence of aerial photography. An extensive complex of timber circles and avenues at Dunragit in the south-west, for example, was only recognised from the air in the early 1990s; it would

31 Map of sites in Chapter 4

originally have been a quite massive construction, on a par with the stone monuments at Calanais in Lewis, or Stenness in Orkney.

The larger henges seem to have had more than simply local significance. The pottery found on these sites includes styles such as Grooved Ware which are replicated from Orkney to Stonehenge. At least the elite members of society seem, therefore, to have had much wider-ranging contacts than we might commonly suppose. Quite how these cultural values spread from place to place is something of a mystery. Common religious beliefs, associated with the sun and moon, and perhaps social bonds of kinship or marriage between ruling groups, probably played a crucial part.

By aligning these arrangements of stones and timbers on the moon, the sun and the stars, chiefs or priests could link their own power to the rhythms and cycles of the natural world. The sun or moon rising over a particular setting of stones or timbers during ritual performances could make it seem that the heavens were tamed and predictable: celestial endorsement for earthly rulers. Some authors have taken this idea rather further, suggesting that highly precise astronomical alignments were encoded in the settings of stones and posts. Such ideas are largely unproveable, but most archaeologists would now accept that observation of the heavens was an important part of the activities carried out at henges and stone circles.

Henges and related monuments have sometimes been compared to medieval cathedrals. Like these later structures, henges could have taken generations to build and could remain in use for hundreds of years. Their architecture embodied an elaborate and widely shared symbolism intimately bound up with the world view and religious beliefs of the societies that built them. Although intended for communal worship, Christian cathedrals were also used for the burial of powerful individuals; as was the case for many henge monuments. We should be wary of stretching such an analogy too far, but it does at least suggest some of the complexities that might lie behind the sacred places of the later Neolithic.

CLEAVEN DYKE, PERTHSHIRE (17)
PRIVATE OWNERSHIP
NO 154 409 (NORTH-WEST END)

How to get there
The Cleaven Dyke is best approached from the main A93 road between Perth and Blairgowrie, where it cuts across the monument. It is not immediately obvious where to park, but if you stop about 700m north of the junction with A984 you should see the distinctive mound heading off at right angles to the road in both directions.

A line across the landscape
The history of communal ritual monuments in Scotland starts with the very first farming communities. One of the earliest and largest ceremonial sites in Scotland has been appreciated only relatively recently. For many years the 1½ mile (2.3km) long bank with widely-spaced flanking ditches, known as the Cleaven Dyke, was thought to be a Roman work, part of the military complex associated with the nearby fort at Inchtuthil. However, recent excavation has shown that it is in fact a huge Neolithic ceremonial monument, built around 3500 BC. Far from being a Roman frontier work, this monument, close to the junction of the Rivers Tay and Isla, would have been many centuries old even at the time of Skara Brae and Maes Howe.

It is hard to appreciate the scale and setting of the Cleaven Dyke today, as much of it is shrouded in dense conifer woodland. However, it is possible to walk along the whole upstanding section of the hump-backed bank, mostly around 10m broad and 2m high (the last couple of hundred metres at the eastern end have been ploughed flat and lie just below the ploughsoil of an arable field).

Processional ways
The elongated enclosure formed by the ditches on either side of the central mound relate the Cleaven Dyke to a group of early ritual sites known as cursus monuments. These have long been known far to the south, for example in Wessex around Stonehenge, but have only recently been recognised as a

major ritual tradition in Scotland. Cursuses can extend for several kilometres and represent major building projects which probably brought together large numbers of people. They contain deposits of pottery and other goods, sometimes even human remains, but they do not appear to have been primarily designed as burial monuments. Most cursuses, however, lack the central mound seen at the Cleaven Dyke (although since many have been totally ploughed out above ground level, many such mounds may have been lost).

The living mound

Excavation has shown that the Cleaven Dyke was built in a series of segments, possibly over many generations. The earliest part seems to be an oval mound at the north-west end, which may well result from an accumulation of early burial monuments. Subsequently a tail of soil and turf was added to create a long mound. From then on short lengths of bank and ditch were built at intervals.

Rites of union

There is no plausible utilitarian explanation for structures like the Cleaven Dyke. Its construction presumably embodied deeply held spiritual or religious beliefs. It was probably built by large groups of people coming together at various important times in the calendar, or in the life of the community. It is possible that this process of co-operation and communal effort between people from otherwise dispersed farming settlements, was more important than the resulting monument, impressive as that would no doubt have been.

BALLOCHMYLE, EAST AYRSHIRE (18)
PRIVATE OWNERSHIP
NS 511 255

How to get there

Driving south east along the A76, carry on for about 1¼ miles (2km) past Mauchline. Take the turning south opposite Ballochmyle Golf Course and park by the gate, about 180m along the road. Cross the stile and follow the footpath. The carvings occupy a large expanse of vertical rock-face somewhat shrouded by overhanging trees on the opposite side of the burn (take care not to touch the carvings; they are extremely fragile).

The rock canvas

While the Cleaven Dyke was a wholly artificial construction, other sacred sites focused on natural features of the landscape. The rock carvings at Ballochmyle, only discovered in the mid-1980s, represent one of the largest collections in Britain (32). Although notoriously difficult to date, such carvings originated well before 3000

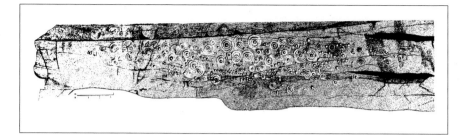

32 Ballochmyle, East Ayrshire; a sample of the carvings

BC, and may have continued to be carved as late as 2000 BC. It is usually difficult or impossible to date individual sets of carving, and Ballochmyle is no exception. Clearly, however, this was a place of some importance, possibly over a protracted period of time, as the carvings seem to belong to more than one episode.

A shared palette

The carvings comprise a wide range of motifs, ranging from simple circular depressions known as cup-marks, to more elaborate geometric designs, set on two adjacent rock panels. Similar carvings are found right across south-west Scotland and indeed along the Atlantic coasts of Europe to Brittany and Portugal. In Scotland they are found on outcrops of rock, often on the fringes of the lands settled in prehistory, as well as on standing stones, or even incorporated into burial monuments as at Balnauran of Clava (see Chapter 3).

Some, particularly the circular cups, rings and rays, may have represented the sun and stars. Or perhaps the commonly recurring patterns are translations in stone of hallucinogenic phenomena experienced by intoxicated shamen. It has even been suggested that they may represent crude maps, the cups and rings representing houses, henges and other monuments. Whatever their precise meaning (and it probably varied greatly over such wide areas and so many centuries), they often seem to have been carved at territorial boundaries, where the farmed lands gave way to the untamed wildscape of hill and loch.

RING OF BRODGAR, ORKNEY (MAINLAND) (19)
HISTORIC SCOTLAND
HY 294 134

How to get there

Take the B9055 to the north from the main road between Kirkwall and Stromness. You can't miss the standing stones as they loom up on your left after about 1 mile (1.5km).

The sacred landscape

The largest and most impressive of all the monuments of Orkney is the henge known as the Ring of Brodgar, sited on the low neck of land which creeps between the lochs of Harray and Stenness (*colour plate 8*). The interplay of sea and sky creates a remarkably serene and isolated atmosphere for a site which was in fact set at the very heart of Neolithic Orkney. Several chambered tombs, including Maes Howe, lie close by, along with standing stones, later burial mounds, and the neighbouring but smaller henge known as the Stones of Stenness (see below). This concentration of ritual monuments is unparalleled anywhere else in Orkney. This was clearly a place of considerable importance in the spiritual life of Neolithic Orcadians.

Encircled stones

Dominating all else is the perfect circle of 27 graceful slim standing stones, the sole standing remnants of an original array of 60. Most stand well above head-height and some are up to 4.5m high. The stones are set in only a few metres from the surrounding ditch, which is equally impressive at 9m wide and 3m deep, cut through solid rock, and enclosing an area of around 110m across. Two opposing entrances run across causeways in the north-west and south-east. Oddly, there is no trace of the external bank.

It has been estimated that it would have taken around 80,000 man hours to dig out the ditch at Brodgar. That is around twice as long as to build the Maes Howe tomb, yet even this figure takes no account of the effort involved in hewing, transporting and erecting the standing stones.

The interior of this vast enclosure has never been excavated so nothing much can be said about the activities which might have taken place within it (*33*). For that we have to look to its near neighbour, the Stones of Stenness.

STENNESS, ORKNEY (MAINLAND) (20)
HISTORIC SCOTLAND
HY 306 125

How to get there

By the time you reach the Ring of Brodgar, you have already passed the Stones of Stenness. They stand by the roadside, just around 500m north of the junction with the main Kirkwall to Stromness road.

The first henge?

Of the original circle of 12 stones, only five now remain, standing up to 5m high (*34*). The surrounding ditch is over 7m wide and 2m deep (although much silted-up today) with an overall diameter of around 45m. Although not quite on the

Above: 33 Rituals at the Ring of
Brodgar, artist's impression

Right: 34 A visit to the Stones of
Stenness, Orkney, 1906

same scale as the Ring of Brodgar, this would nonetheless have been an imposing monument in its day. Excavations in the 1970s showed that it was built around 3000 BC; the same period as the nearby settlement at Barnhouse, and Skara Brae, some 6 miles (10km) distant (see Chapter 2) and very close in date to Maes Howe. This is also one of the earliest dates for a henge anywhere in Britain.

Ritual feasts

At the centre of the monument was a large stone setting, much like a domestic hearth but blown up hugely in scale. The ditch contained bones of cattle, sheep, wolves and dogs; presumably remnants of sacrifice and feasting within the henge.

It is tempting to see a progression from the tomb at Maes Howe to the Stones of Stenness, and finally to the Ring of Brodgar; each perhaps built by subsequent generations in a effort to outdo their predecessors. As yet, however, archaeology cannot provide dating evidence sufficiently detailed to test such speculations.

CALANAIS (CALLANISH), LEWIS, WESTERN ISLES (21)
HISTORIC SCOTLAND
NB 213 330

How to get there

The Calanais Stones are visible from some way off on a prominent ridge overlooking the township of Calanais, above Loch Roag on the west coast of Lewis. The site is reached by a minor road sign-posted from the A958. There is a spacious car-park and visitor centre at the end of the minor road, from which you approach the stones on foot.

Temple of the Isles

The main setting at Calanais is one of the best known and most evocative ancient monuments in Scotland, adorning the covers of numerous books and a multitude of postcards (*colour plate 9*). Unlike Stenness and Brodgar, Calanais has no henge. Instead an impressive array of standing stones have been choreographed into an elegant and complex cross-shaped arrangement unparalleled elsewhere in Britain (*35*).

Early visitors

The presence of such an imposing monument in such an apparently grim peatland environment has attracted much curiosity over the centuries. The writer and traveller Martin Martin, writing in 1716, was greatly impressed by the 'number, bigness and order' of the stones and was told that this 'was a place appointed for worship in the time of heathenism, and that the chief druid or

35 The Calanais
Stones, Lewis

priest stood near the big stone in the centre, from whence he addressed himself
to the people that surrounded him'. Druids aside, this remains as good an
interpretation as any.

A gathering of stones

The central monolith, almost 5m high, is surrounded by a near-circular ring of
13 standing stones, about 12m in diameter. This circle is approached from the
north by a double avenue of stones, 80m long, and with shorter single lines
leading off to the east, west and south to form the arms of a great cross. Each of
the stones could have been quarried fairly locally, but it would have taken a great
many people (probably at least 30-40) to shift the largest stones any distance over
the rugged, rocky terrain, and to erect them on the ridge.

Numerous subtleties are built in to the basic arrangement; for example the
avenue stones are graded in height, with the highest at either end and the
lowest towards the middle, and the stones on the western side of the monument
are generally smaller than those on the east (perhaps echoing the left/right
symbolism at Skara Brae (see Chapter 2)). It can be a little difficult for the visitor
get to grips with the original design, as the modern path brings you in at the

wrong' end. It was probably always the intention that you should approach from the far end, flanked by the stones of the double avenue.

Variations on a theme

Although the cruciform plan of Calanais is unique, it seems to be a characteristic of the great ritual centres of Neolithic Britain that no two were exactly alike. Instead each seems to re-work the basic building blocks, of stones, ditches, banks and timbers to form a unique and individual expression of shared values, symbols and traditions.

A history in stone

Excavations in the 1980s gave some insights into the development of the monument. Around 3000 BC it seems that the ridge was given over to arable ground, although there are tantalising hints of earlier, dismantled structures on the site. Between 2900-2600 BC, however, the stones were dragged into place and set up to form the main elements of the monument as we see it today. This dating places Calanais only slightly later than the Stones of Stenness, and rather earlier than the great stone circle at Stonehenge. The builders used Grooved Ware pottery, closely similar to the types found at these other centres.

Shortly afterwards a small, otherwise undistinguished, chambered tomb was erected in the centre of the circle, somewhat uncomfortably squashed between the central stone and the ring. This slightly incongruous addition may not have been part of the original design but it was apparently built soon after the circle; perhaps even housing one or more of the builders. The tomb was apparently in use for several centuries thereafter, judging from the variety of pottery types represented in the debris cast out from the chamber when it was ransacked and despoiled around 2000-1750 BC.

Satellite stones

Less well known than the main setting are the numerous other megalithic monuments in the vicinity, including at least three other stone circles, various lesser alignments and single stones. As you drive towards the main site from Stornoway you can see two of the other circles in the fields to your left. These are well worth a visit in their own right. Taken as a group, the profusion and scale of the monuments around Calanais suggest that this was a place of some importance: a regional centre around which a congregation of smaller monuments was built.

Quite why Calanais should have emerged as the key regional centre, however, is something of a mystery. Before the sea drowned the low-lying ground and peat engulfed the fields, this would have been a fairly rich area for early farming communities: pollen preserved in the peat shows that the Neolithic islanders grew crops in the vicinity before the climate turned against them and the soils disappeared below a blanket of peat (the stones themselves were part-buried in over a metre of peat until the local landowner, Sir James Mathieson had them dug out in 1857). Yet other areas were more fertile, and North Uist, with its large concentration of chambered tombs (see Barpa Langass in Chapter 3) seems to have been the focus for earlier expressions of ritual life.

Stones and stars

Over the centuries countless scholars and laymen alike have pondered the nature of the rituals carried out at sites like Calanais. 'Astro-archaeologists', followers of Professor Alexander Thom, claim that the stones formed a prehistoric lunar observatory. They believe that alignments traceable between the various elements of such monuments relate to the movement of the sun, stars and (particularly at Calanais) the moon. Others say that, at specific times within the lunar cycle (every 18.6 years) observers in the stone avenue can watch the moon seem to glide along the hills of the Clisham range to the south, disappear for a time, only to re-emerge even brighter between the stones.

Critics of such theories point out that the irregularity and great size of the stones means that numerous alignments will always be preserved in a megalithic monument by chance alone. Erosion and displacement of the stones further hamper any attempt to evaluate theories based on more detailed measurements. Nonetheless, precocious temple of astronomy or not, observation of the heavens was undoubtedly an important part of the rituals performed at Calanais. The sight of the moon rising and setting year after year in predictable interplay with the stones and the landscape must have been deeply reassuring for communities whose very existence was dependant on the whims of nature.

MACHRIE MOOR, ARRAN (22)
HISTORIC SCOTLAND
NR 911 324 (FOR THE LARGEST CIRCLE)

How to get there

The footpath onto the moor is sign-posted from the A841. Park in the passing place about 300m north of Tormore, and 200m before the bridge over the Machrie Water. Allow a decent length of time to explore this complex which is strung out over an extensive area of moorland. The furthest stone circles and hut circles are a 1¼ mile (2km) trudge from the main road.

The relict landscape

Six stone circles lie quite close together at the far end of the complex on Machrie Moor. Once you reach the abandoned steading of Moss Farm you are in the right general area. By then, however, you will already have passed the remains of numerous chambered cairns, Later Bronze Age burial cairns and hut circles strewn across the moor.

Assembly on the moors

The cluster of stone circles is reminiscent of that around Calanais, although the Machrie circles are much more concentrated and none has quite the individual impact of the main setting at Calanais. The most visually striking stands around 200m beyond the steading and includes three uprights each around 5.5m high; taller even than the central stone at Calanais (*36*). Strewn around are the fallen slabs that once completed the circle (one has been subject to an abortive attempt to turn it into a pair of mill-stones).

Less than 50m further on lies a much more modest assembly of ten stones forming a ring. This setting was in fact only discovered a few years ago during excavation work on this part of the site, showing how much even well-known sites still have to hide. The stones of this circle seem rather stunted in comparison with Calanais; squat boulders rather than graceful slabs. What is particularly interesting about them, however, is that they overlie much older timber circles, not now visible, which were built around the same time as the stone setting at Calanais.

The main timber circle had around 50 posts up to 2.5m high with a horseshoe-shaped setting of even larger posts inside; a monumental construction that must have rivalled even Calanais in its heyday. A few centuries later a somewhat smaller timber circle was built only 20m or so away, perhaps reflecting the emergence of satellite circles around Calanais.

36 The tallest of the stone circles on Machrie Moor, Arran; note the unfinished mill-stones in the foreground

Veneration and decay

Between the timber and stone circles was a lengthy episode of agricultural use, when we can only surmise that ritual activity shifted to other parts of the moor. It is perhaps this evolution and time depth in the ritual landscape that is the most intriguing feature of the Machrie Moor complex.

TEMPLE WOOD AND KILMARTIN LINEAR CEMETERY, ARGYLL (23-4) HISTORIC SCOTLAND
NR 826 978 (TEMPLE WOOD)

How to get there

The small museum at Kilmartin House on the A816 between Oban and Inverary provides a good introduction to the monuments of Kilmartin Glen. An archaeological trail takes you around a wealth of archaeological monuments. The linear cemetery and Temple Wood stone circle are sign-posted from the main road south of the village.

A monumental landscape

A whole collection of Neolithic and Bronze Age monuments is laid out along the Kilmartin Glen. Together they form a ritual complex that evolved over hundreds of years, on a par with the ritual centres of Orkney, Calanais and Machrie Moor.

Timber to stone

Excavations at Temple Wood in the 1970s uncovered a sequence of activity strikingly similar to that at Machrie Moor. First a circle of timbers was laid out, prior to 3000 BC. This is now marked by a ring of concrete posts. Later a larger circle of twenty-two standing stones was built beside the earlier timber version and for centuries thereafter the site became a focus for burials in small cairns in and around the stones. Finally the whole circle was turned into one great funerary monument by covering it over with stones. Excavation and restoration has left the standing stones clearly visible, as is the later burial cist at the centre of the circle (37).

The linear cemetery

The earliest of the series of tombs that make up the linear cemetery is probably Nether Largie South (NR 828 979). Here a chambered tomb not unlike several described in Chapter 3, has been swallowed up by a later, larger Bronze Age burial mound in which several burials were inserted. The chamber lies open in the centre, although originally it would have been roofed and reached by a passage now lost within the body of the later cairn (38).

37 The central cist at Temple Wood stone circle, Argyll

CAIRNPAPPLE, WEST LOTHIAN (25)
HISTORIC SCOTLAND
NS 987 717

How to get there

Take the minor road south from the centre of Linlithgow for about 3 miles (5km), past Beecraigs Country Park. The site is well sign-posted. A small exhibition is housed in a Nissan hut next to the henge, and a custodian is on hand seasonally to clarify the complexities of the site's history.

The rediscovered hilltop

Cairnpapple Hill, overlooking a huge swathe of central Scotland, is an intuitively fitting location for a major ritual monument (*colour plate 11*). From the hilltop, when the weather is fine, you can see north as far as the summit of Schiehallion in Perthshire, as far west as Goatfell on Arran, and east past Arthur's Seat to the Bass Rock (the views being blighted only by a clump of unsightly radio masts). Yet its importance as a Neolithic regional centre on a par with Calanais or the Stenness complex, was recognised only relatively recently, following excavations by Professor Stuart Piggott in the 1940s. Standing on the bare hilltop today, it is hard to imagine that, when looking for the reputed site of the cairn in 1852, Mr Charles Cowan and friend failed to find it in dense woodland.

As laid out today, a visit to Cairnpapple is rather like wandering through a full-scale archaeological plan. The burial cairn has been reconstructed as a concrete

38 A standing stone covered with cup-and-ring markings, at Nether Largie in the Kilmartin Valley

39 The reconstructed cairn at Cairnpapple with the Iron Age graves in the foreground

bunker into which you can clamber to inspect the reconstructed graves (when new, the cairn was solid earth and stone). The stone and timber holes of various periods were left open after excavation and are conveniently filled with colour-coded gravel to signify which phase they belong to. The effect is odd but quite helpful; a monument to 1940s site interpretation as well as Neolithic ritual (39).

The sacred hilltop

The hilltop setting is most unusual for a henge monument, but may be explained by the earlier history of ritual and burial on the site. Perhaps as early as 3000 BC precious objects were left as offerings on the hill, including fine pottery bowls and stone axe-heads imported from Cumbria and Wales. As times changed the decision was made to build a grand henge monument in the new style. Cairnpapple, with its pre-existing ritual resonances must have seemed a wholly appropriate setting.

The Cairnpapple henge was probably rather later in date than those in the far north and west; perhaps being built around 2500 BC. It was not, however, to be outshone, for this henge was a major construction; demarcated by a ditch 3.5m wide and cut over a metre deep into the rock, with an accompanying external bank. Two wide entrances gave access from both north and south. Inside was an egg-shaped setting of 24 large timber posts (or, less likely, standing stones) and an inner setting of posts or stones.

It has been suggested that the timber circle may have pre-dated the henge proper, as it is not quite concentric and has only one entrance (and even that does not line up exactly with either entrance to the henge). Even if it was earlier, however, it was probably still standing when the henge was built and should be considered as part of the same process of monumentalising the earlier informal sanctity of the hilltop.

While the extraordinary panorama of Neolithic central Scotland would doubtless have made its mark on the psyche of those climbing the hill, once inside the enclosure all this would have disappeared. For when the bank was standing to its full height all you would have been able to see from the henge was sky. Like Calanais, this would have been an ideal place from which to observe the stars.

The return of the dead

The henge does not seem to have been designed as a place of burial, but rather as a place of communal ritual. Yet some time after its construction, perhaps several hundred years later, the function of the monument was to change radically. Firstly a small cairn of stone and clay was built just off centre in the western part of the interior. This was marked at the east end by a large standing stone over 2m high and surrounded by a setting of smaller stones. Underneath was buried at least one adult represented only by the stain of the decayed body, with the remains of wooden objects; one over the face, presumably a mask, and another by the side, perhaps a club or mace. Two pottery vessels, of a type known as beakers probably date the burial to around 2000 BC, some centuries after the construction of the henge. Although this relatively modest cairn was subsequently obscured beneath the later mound, the grave itself is preserved and open to view within the reconstructed concrete dome.

Some time later, this first cairn was replaced and subsumed within the body of a much larger cairn; now replicated by the concrete dome which dominates the site. Whereas the first cairn had sat comfortably within the earlier monument, this new construction, some 15m across and several metres high, with a kerb of massive stone slabs, dominated the interior of the henge, and surely implies that the once communal monument had been usurped for the grave of a prominent individual. Later still, more stone was brought onto the site and used to expand the existing cairn to around twice its diameter. This new cairn, 30m across, overlay the ditch of the henge; confirmation that the original form of the monument was by now incidental to what may now have become a dynastic tomb.

Its hard to escape the conclusion that this was the burial place of powerful people who dominated central Scotland in life as their graves did in death. The labour of perhaps hundreds of people was now marshalled to create successive monuments to a few privileged souls.

BALFARG, FIFE (26)
LOCAL AUTHORITY ARCHAEOLOGICAL TRAIL
NO 280 030

How to get there

The archaeological trail at Balfarg straddles the A92 Kirkcaldy-Cupar road. The starting point, the henge, is sign-posted from the roundabout on which sits a modern fake stone circle (just to get you in the mood). The henge lies in the middle of a modern housing estate, and is not the most evocative of Neolithic sites. Nonetheless, this was once the main ritual centre for this part of Scotland.

A henge in the suburbs

The complex at Balfarg is one of the most accessible places from which to appreciate the scale and integration of the Neolithic ritual landscape. After excavation to make way for the modern houses, several parts of the complex were restored and equipped with information boards. The guide booklet (Balfarg, by Gordon Barclay) is also perhaps the best introduction to the Neolithic of lowland Scotland.

The henge is a large arena, 60m across, once enclosed by a substantial bank and ditch through which passed a narrow western entrance causeway. The stubby posts which surround the interior today mark the positions of massive timber uprights, up to 4m high. Later an inner stone setting was added, of which only two are still preserved. Inside were found the remnants of various rituals, involving feasting, sacrifice and the smashing of fine pottery vessels.

As at Cairnpapple the evolution of this complex over the centuries led from communal ritual to individual burial. A huge slab towards the centre of the henge originally covered the burial of a young person laid to rest with a beaker pot and a flint knife. Quite some effort had gone into this burial, judging from the size of the stone, and the prestigious location suggests a funeral of some importance. If this youth was a member of the ruling elite, it would suggest that power was inherited rather than won through personal prowess.

Around the houses

A marked path from the henge leads to other reconstructed elements of the complex; including an earlier timber enclosure seemingly used for the exposure of the dead prior to burial, and a stone circle. Many other graves, mounds and ritual enclosures have been engulfed by the housing development.

LOANHEAD OF DAVIOT, ABERDEENSHIRE (27)
HISTORIC SCOTLAND
NJ 747 288

How to get there

Follow the signs from the main A920 road a few miles north-west of Oldmeldrum. There is a small car park at the site.

Sitting stones

The stone circle which forms the main focus of Loanhead of Daviot has a remarkable feature that distinguishes it from the other stone circles mentioned so far. At the south-west part of the circle a massive stone slab lies on its side, flanked by two uprights. This arrangement is the defining feature of a group of around 100 monuments found only in and around Aberdeenshire, and commonly called recumbent stone circles (40).

Framing the moon

It has been suggested that this arrangement of stones formed a frame from which observations could be made of the moon, in effect creating a false horizon. This idea seems to tally with the setting of these monuments, usually in prominent locations where an uninterrupted view of the heavens would have been available. It is unfortunate that the thick-set trees around Loanhead of Daviot obscure its original open landscape setting.

40 Loanhead of Daviot, Aberdeenshire, from the air; the recumbent stone circle is on the right

Regional links

Generally the stones are graded in height with the largest to the south-west, either side of the recumbent stone. This arrangement is reminiscent of the tombs at Balnauran of Clava (see Chapter 3) and elsewhere in the Inverness area. Indeed the distribution of recumbent stone circles is mutually exclusive with that of henges and Clava-type cairns, perhaps suggesting that they were all contemporary regional variants on the same theme.

The recumbent stone circle was the earliest major structure to be built on the site. It may have been built around 2500 BC or earlier, judging from the remnants of pottery placed with cremated human remains and piles of stone around some of the uprights. Later almost the whole of the interior was filled by a low, almost flat, ring cairn; a solid circle of boulders enclosing an open central space around 4m across. Under this were the remains of cremation burials. As at Cairnpapple and Balfarg, a site seemingly built for communal ritual had turned into what was essentially a cemetery.

Burnt offerings

Just next to the stone circle, is a smaller enclosure formed by a circular ditch and stone bank. This contained the cremated remains of upwards of thirty people, some within simple graves and others buried in upturned pottery urns. Among them in the centre, was a man, only partly cremated, seemingly clasping a stone pendant. This may have been the primary burial around which the later cremations were placed.

Although the use of the complex may have begun at the same time as the great henge monuments, the pottery buried here shows that Loanhead of Daviot was used as a cemetery for many centuries, well into second millennium BC.

CROFTMORAIG, PERTHSHIRE (28)
PRIVATE OWNERSHIP
NN 797 472

How to get there
The stone circle is clearly visible immediately to the right of the A827, about 2 miles (3km) north of Kenmore on the way to Aberfeldy. You should seek permission before entering.

Local centres
Not all stone circles were regional centres. Some seem to have served more modest communities. One such is Croftmoraig, a double circle of stones with

41 Croftmoraig, Perthshire

various outliers; one of a number of relatively small megalithic monuments set along Strathtay (*41*).

Excavations in the 1960s showed, however, that these sites too could have lengthy histories. The earliest activity is not now visible. It comprised a horseshoe-shaped setting of timber posts, later replaced by a similar setting of 8 large boulders. These stones, some about 2m high, form the inner part of the monument. The outer ring was added later.

HILL O' MANY STANES, MID CLYTH, CAITHNESS (29)
HISTORIC SCOTLAND
ND 294 384

How to get there
The site lies just beside a minor road sign-posted from the main A9 around 8¾ miles (14km) south of Wick.

Ritual rows
This slightly twee name describes a remarkable series of stone rows set on a barren Caithness hillside (*colour plate 10*). The obvious care which has gone into its construction combined with utter lack of any obvious purpose renders this one of Scotland's most mystifying ancient monuments. The site has never been excavated and cannot be closely dated. Nevertheless, the business of manoeuvring blocks of stone into elaborate settings firmly links it to the wider megalithic traditions of the Neolithic, and suggests that it may be a local variant of the kinds of ritual centre represented by the henges and stone circles.

A Neolithic calculator?
In all the monument comprises over 250 rather stunted upright stones set into 22 rows arranged broadly from north to south, spreading out in a fan-like formation down the hillside. None exceed waist-height. It has been suggested that the intricate fan-shape of this and similar sites was intended to help chart the movements of the moon over both its 4-week and 18.6-year cycle. The mathematics involved are extremely complicated and it is perhaps doubtful whether the rows were laid out with anything like the precision required. Nonetheless, some more basic form of lunar observation may well have been involved in the rituals performed around these stones.

Contact or coincidence?
Stone rows are not at all common in Scotland, and the dozen or so examples in the far north evoke parallels with the rather more visually impressive stone rows at sites like Carnac in Brittany and on Dartmoor.

5

Forts and farms of the Iron Age

By around 1000 BC the great megalithic monuments of the Neolithic and Bronze Age had long since ceased to be built. Even if some were still venerated and visited, these monuments, and the old gods they served, were now firmly part of the past. The communities of Iron Age Scotland seem to have seen their world in radically different ways and the monuments they have left us are of a quite different character.

Of all the various periods of Scottish prehistory it is probably the Iron Age, from around 700 BC until the Roman invasion around AD 80, which gave rise to the greatest number of monuments still visible in the countryside today. In contrast to earlier periods, it is structures associated with daily living, rather than with death and religion, that dominate: these can take the form of isolated houses, rambling villages, and enclosed, even fortified settlements (42). This was also a period of marked region-alisation with different types of structure predominating in different areas. The north and west in particular developed its own distinctive forms of architecture, notably the broch towers, and these are described in Chapter 6.

Even within the south and east, however, there were differences from region to region. Some were dominated by crannogs, or islet settlements (see 9), some by timber roundhouses (43), and others by brooding hilltop enclosures (see 7). Yet almost everywhere, Iron Age people, unlike their Neolithic and Bronze Age ancestors, shared a common preoccupation with house and home, and huge attention and effort was lavished on the building and maintenance of elaborate houses and enclosures. This emphasis on domestic life seems even to have been at the expense of elaborate burials and formal religious monuments, which are extremely rare during the period. Despite this, recent finds have provided some

42 Map of sites in Chapter 5

insights into the burial rites afforded at least to a few select members of society. In 2001, a grave was found at Newbridge, just outside Edinburgh, which contained a complete two-wheeled cart or chariot dating to around 450 BC. Although there were no other grave goods, and the body itself had all but vanished over time, the burial rite inextricably links this site with a concentration of Iron Age chariot burials in East Yorkshire and northern France. In fact, the most direct parallels come from Belgian sites of the same period, providing a tantalising glimpse into the long-range contacts of Iron Age Scottish communities. Another unexpected find, from Alloa in 2003, revealed the burial of an adult male with sword and spear, dating to the later part of the Iron Age. But despite these occasionally spectacular exceptions, it is clear that most of the dead of Iron Age Scotland were disposed of in ways that evade archaeological discovery.

Elsewhere, we can occasionally catch a glimpse of Iron Age religious life, for instance the wooden figurine recovered from a bog at Ballachulish (see pl. 8), or burials of human and animal remains beneath the floors of certain northern roundhouses, but few specifically religious or funerary sites have been found.

The monuments that survive best in the south and east, however, are the massively constructed hillforts. The earth and stone ramparts and accompanying ditches of these sites can be seen on hilltops all across the uplands of southern

43 Timber roundhouses were a common feature of the Iron Age in the south and east, but they are rarely visible on the surface today. This artist's impression gives some idea of the scale and construction of these vanished buildings

Scotland, and more sporadically north of the Forth and Clyde. Much of the settlement of the Iron Age was concentrated on the arable lowlands, but farming over countless generations has obliterated all surface traces of the fragile timber buildings of the Iron Age farmers. Although the remains of settlement in the lowlands can often be detected from the air (*44*), there are few sites in these areas that can still be visited today. Bear in mind then, that impressive as the standing remains are, they are only a tiny fraction of what was originally there.

EILDON HILL NORTH, SCOTTISH BORDERS (30)
PRIVATE OWNERSHIP
NT 554 328

How to get there
Head south from the centre of Melrose on the B6359. The path to the hillfort is sign-posted from there and involves a bracing uphill hike. The site, and the views, are well worth the effort.

44 Many major lowland sites of
the Iron Age survive only below
ground. Some, like this large, multi–
ditched East Lothian fort, show up
as 'cropmarks' from the air, when
soil and crop conditions are right

Bronze Age forts

For many years it was thought that Scotland's largest hillforts, including Eildon
Hill North, and Traprain Law in East Lothian, were the tribal capitals of the
peoples who faced the Roman invaders in the first century AD. While this may
be so, both were also occupied much earlier, from the Later Bronze Age if not
before.

The hill-town

Eildon Hill North is the highest of three peaks towering above modern Melrose
(*45*). The summit of the hill is encircled by over 3 miles (5km) of ramparts
enclosing an immense area of around 40 acres (16ha), densely packed with
foundation platforms for prehistoric roundhouses. Each platform was laboriously
scooped out of the natural rock to create a level surface on which a turf or
timber-walled house could be built. These foundations are quite obvious as you
walk around the hill, but it can be difficult to appreciate the sheer numbers and
density of housing that they represent.

It is possible that the hundreds of house platforms were built up over many
generations through the periodic visits of a shifting population. Once they were
built, however, these platforms would have formed convenient house stances for
all subsequent inhabitants, and fresh platforms would presumably only have been
built if all the others were occupied. Since there were at least 300 platforms on

the hill (and possibly up to 600 house stances originally), it would appear that, at certain times, a great many people were in residence. If we were to assume an extended family of around 10 people per house, then the minimum of 300 houses would have sheltered 3000 people: a more generous figure for the number of houses might give up to 6000 people. This is a quite staggering figure for such a remote period: no population centre of comparable size was to exist in Scotland for well over a thousand years (46).

In search of the Selgovae

Eildon Hill North is traditionally associated with the pre-Roman tribe known as the Selgovae, who were recorded by the Roman geographer, Ptolemy. Recent excavations have shown, however, that occupation on the hill goes back to around 1000 BC; well into the Bronze Age, and about 1000 years before we hear of the Selgovae. This does not necessarily mean that the houses all date to this early period, since only a tiny fraction of these have been excavated and dated. Nonetheless, there is little evidence from the limited excavations for a significant population on the hill in the period just before the Romans arrived.

The Roman presence

The dominant landscape position of Eildon Hill North, which was so attractive to the status-hungry native population, was equally important to the Roman army, though for rather different reasons. In the first century AD the massive fort of Newstead (known to the Romans as Trimontium after the three Eildon peaks) was established in the shadow of the hill, and a signal tower was built on the summit to send and receive signals, or perhaps to keep an eye on the movement of people in the area. If Eildon Hill North was still a thriving native stronghold when the Romans arrived, it appears that it was soon emptied of its native inhabitants.

On the west part of the summit of the hill you can still see the small, circular, ditched enclosure (about 11m in diameter) which surrounded the timber signal station. Inside stood a two-storey rectangular tower. Finds of Roman tile from the summit suggest that it had a tiled roof. Certainly it would have been a stark and imposing structure, crowning the hilltop amid the ruins of the abandoned native fort.

Retaking the hill

Oddly, despite the lack of pre-Roman Iron Age activity, there seems to have been renewed native occupation during the Roman period, from the second to fourth centuries AD. Roman coins and pottery, together with some more recent dating evidence from small-scale excavations, suggest that some of the platforms were re-occupied at this time.

It seems inconceivable that the Roman army would have tolerated a fortified native settlement above their own fort and civilian settlement at Newstead, so

45 Eildon Hill North from
the air

how can we explain the presence of these late houses? It is possible that the hill
had become a religious site, surrounded by the redundant defences. Or, perhaps
more likely, the occupation may represent the periodic reclamation of the old
stronghold by the local people at those times when the Roman army was
entrenched far to the south, at Hadrian's Wall.

TRAPRAIN LAW, EAST LOTHIAN (31)
LOCAL AUTHORITY OWNERSHIP
NT 580 746

How to get there
Traprain Law is sign-posted from the A1 between Haddington and East Linton.
Use the car park on the north side of the hill, where there are also information
boards, and follow the marked footpath to the summit.

Eildon's twin?
Just as Eildon Hill commands the Tweed valley for miles around, the great volcanic
crag of Traprain Law dominates the sprawling arable lands of East Lothian's
coastal plain, visible from the Pentland Hills to the west, the Lammermuirs to

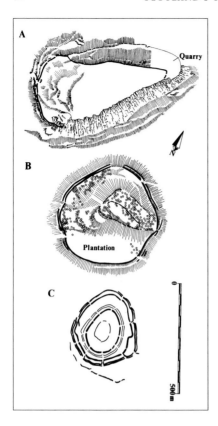

46 This plan shows the three major hillforts of (a) Traprain Law (b) Eildon Hill North, and (c) the Brown Caterthun, to the same scale

the south and Fife to the north (*colour plate 12*). From the first settlers onwards, anyone who wanted to stake a claim to this land could find no better base.

Before visiting Traprain Law it is worth stopping off at the lay-by and tourist information centre on the A1 between Haddington and East Linton. From there you can look south across the River Tyne and see the whole mass of Traprain Law laid out before you. Most obvious of all at first glance is the gigantic bite take out of the north-east side of the hill by a modern quarry (*46*). After thousands of years of habitation and veneration of the site, the contribution of our own age was to attempt its removal. Thankfully, the quarry is now disused, and has itself now become a piece of industrial archaeology.

Looking at the north face of the hill it is easy to discern the remains of the successive stone and earth ramparts emerging from the quarry, quite high up the hillside, and snaking along the contours to the west. On Traprain itself, the ramparts are best seen on the west side of the hill. A series of wide entrances, through which paths pass on their way to the summit, are particularly striking. The west shoulder of the hill also contains some of the flattest ground, particularly on a large plateau just off the summit, where excavations were carried out in the early part of this century. Although the internal buildings are much less obvious than at Eildon, these excavations showed that layer upon layer of fragmentary stone and timber houses survive under the turf.

A stroll around the summit gives an idea of the power and status that control of this site would have given. Its dominance in the landscape is hard to exaggerate, with views over an immense area of land and sea.

Temple or fort?

Traprain Law was inhabited, or at least visited, for thousands of years. By around 1500 BC it was already a place of burial: the rather denuded remains of what might be a stone burial cairn of this period are to be found just east of the trig point on the summit. Also from this broad period are the remains of a complex series of rock carvings. Several large panels, carved on the living rock, were found during quarrying in the 1930s. Unfortunately, these elaborate carvings, comprising cup-and-ring markings and hatched linear designs, were mercilessly blown up and survive only in the form of plaster casts in the stores of the National Museums of Scotland. Excavations in 2004, however, identified a further, smaller panel on the south side of the hill, and it seems likely that more remain to be found. After 1000 BC, there is evidence of a more permanent presence: the earliest ramparts semmingly have their origins in this period, although they were re-built and re-aligned on numerous occasions. The houses revealed by excavation seem to show a continuing dense occupation for centuries thereafter.

Towns or fairs?

What brought these huge numbers of people together on hilltops such as Traprain Law and Eildon Hill North? Conventionally they have been seen as hill towns; permanent settlements for large communities, housing the tribal aristocracy and their retinue of warriors, priests and craftsmen, as well as the lesser orders. Impressive as these hills are, however, they are also cold and wind-blasted, and would have necessitated a thankless uphill trudge at the end of each day's labour in the surrounding fields. Is it then realistic to see them as permanently settled hill-towns?

Perhaps, rather than permanent settlements, they should be seen rather as seasonal meeting-places, sites of festivals or fairs, where large groups of people would congregate at specific times. Such special places, often with a small permanent population of priests, craftsmen or local nobility, existed until quite recently, for example in certain Native American communities.

Friends of the Empire

While Eildon Hill has been associated with the Selgovae, Traprain Law has long been seen as the capital of the inhabitants of Lothian: a tribe known as the Votadini (who subsequently emerged into history as the post-Roman kingdom of Gododdin). The absence of Roman military establishments in East Lothian, east of modern Musselburgh, together with the large quantities of Roman goods which found their way onto Traprain Law, have led to the theory that the Votadini were allies of Rome.

It is easy to imagine how the interests of a prosperous tribal dynasty based in East Lothian might have been served by such an alliance. So long as they kept their distance, the Roman army would have provided valuable insurance against aggression from troublesome neighbours. The prestige of Votadinian chiefs may also have been enhanced by their access to exotic Roman goods. This may well have been a deal well worth the inevitable taxes demanded to support the Roman garrisons.

Troubled times

Deep layers of settlement debris containing Roman pottery show continued occupation at Traprain Law through the third and fourth centuries AD, at a time when the northern limit of the Roman Empire was firmly fixed far to the south. Towards the end of this period, however, things seem to have taken a turn for the worse. Around AD 400 a new enclosing rampart was built to impressive specifications. At 4m wide, with stone facings inside and out, this was the most imposing rampart ever to grace the site, and the only one suggestive of serious military intent. Its remains are particularly impressive on the western approach to the summit.

If this was all that had happened, we might be tempted to interpret it as simply the whim of a new war-leader, keen to stamp his mark on the ancient hilltop. But this was a period when Roman sources suggest increasingly unstable conditions as the whole edifice of Roman Britain shuddered into terminal decline. Within a few years, decades at most, Traprain Law had been entirely abandoned, never to be resettled. Perhaps the last rampart was an act of desperation after all.

The Traprain treasure

At around the same time as the last rampart was built, an extraordinary collection of Roman silverware, including bowls, spoons, flagons, dishes and plates (11), was cut up and buried in a pit, under the floor of one of the abandoned houses. This was richly decorative material, awash with Mediterranean motifs such as dolphins and leaping panthers. Quite what these images meant to the inhabitants of the Lothian hilltop we will never know. The silverware probably originated as a diplomatic gift from the Roman authorities in the south or from trade links, although we cannot rule out the possibility that it was loot from a particularly successful raid beyond Hadrian's Wall.

Equally problematic is how such wealth came to be sliced up and buried in a pit. It is usually suggested that the hoard was buried for safety, although its fragmentary condition is strikingly reminiscent of prehistoric ritual offerings, where bronze swords and other prized objects were bent or broken and cast into pools or bogs to appease the gods. Both explanations might suggest stressful times.

TAP O' NOTH, ABERDEENSHIRE (32)
PRIVATE OWNERSHIP
NJ 484 293

How to get there
Take the track just west of Scurdague Farm on the A971, then head uphill. The distance from road to summit is about half-a-mile (1km) and is not to be undertaken lightly.

Hidden houses
At over 560m high, Tap o' Noth is the second highest hillfort in Scotland and probably also the largest. Although much of the 52 acres (21ha) enclosed by the outermost rampart seems fairly featureless to the casual eye, there are many platforms, similar to those on Eildon Hill North though usually less distinct. Some are probably quarries for the ramparts, but others may be house foundations.

Glass walls?
Large though the outer wall is in extent, it's physical remains are not overwhelmingly impressive. The same cannot be said, however, of the massive stone wall that encircles the summit of the hill, which is over 6m wide and over 3m high. When first built, it was probably double that height, surrounding an oval area around 100m by 40m.

Along the wall have been found lumps of glassy material known as vitrified stone. This material is produced by the effects of intense and prolonged heat which causes the stones of the rampart to melt and fuse together. It is quite common on Iron Age forts, particularly in the east and north-east. Quite how such intense heat came to be applied to these walls has been a matter of long-running debate.

Blazing hills
What vitrified forts have in common is that their walls were formed of stone supported by a timber framework or core. It used to be thought that vitrified forts had been fired deliberately, to provide extra strength. In fact vitrification of the wall core would have greatly weakened the rampart and made it highly unstable. Nor was vitrification the incidental by-product of siege or battle, for experiments have shown that only carefully laid and maintained fires could have achieved the required temperatures for long enough.

Vitrification was, it seems, a deliberate act of premeditated destruction carried out either in the aftermath of war, or once the forts had been abandoned. The effect of such a massive structure as the Tap o' Noth citadel burning brightly against the skyline for days must have been spectacular indeed. Whoever burnt it would certainly have made their point.

THE BROWN AND WHITE CATERTHUNS, ANGUS (33-4)
HISTORIC SCOTLAND
NO 555 668 (BROWN CATERTHUN) AND NO 547 660 (WHITE CATERTHUN)

How to get there
From the A94 (Aberdeen - Dundee) turn off at the exit marked Careston. Follow the minor road for around 3 miles (5km) until you arrive at a T-junction. Turn right. After half-a-mile (1km) the road forks. Take the left fork and the next left is sign-posted for the Caterthuns. There is a car park with information boards on the minor road which runs between the two hills. Tracks lead from there to each of the sites.

Twin towns?
The Brown and White Caterthuns crown neighbouring hills, both commanding sweeping views across mile after mile of prime Angus farmland. The White Caterthun is so-called because of the huge mass of stone rubble (debris from the fort) that caps its summit (*colour plate 13*). The Brown presumably takes it name from its covering of heather. Contrasting colours apart, these two forts have striking similarities in design.

The ruins of the wall atop the White Caterthun are spread to a width of over 20m. Like that at Tap o' Noth it seems to be partly vitrified, suggesting that it was held together by a timber frame. Its original dimensions must have been impressive, although without excavation it is hard to give more than a broad estimate of perhaps 10m wide by 5-6m high wide. Inside are the foundations of several rectangular buildings and what appears to be a dried-up well. The great stone fort was probably the last major construction on either of the hills, and could date to the last centuries BC or the first half of the first millennium AD.

Downslope lie the remains of a series of earlier earthen ramparts, almost identical to those on the neighbouring Brown Caterthun. Recent excavations on the Brown Caterthun mean that its history of construction is rather better known, although the similarities between the two sites are such that they probably developed in parallel.

The Brown Caterthun has at least six ramparts belonging to three groups, and seems to have gradually expanded through time (*46*). The innermost is a simple oval enclosure on the summit, which marks the position of a 'box' rampart, originally faced inside and out with a timber palisade. It was probably built some time around 700 BC although it is not closely dated. The middle group comprises three close-set ramparts (the middle one of these is little more than a terrace), of which the innermost is the most substantial rampart on the hill, up to 7m wide. These date to around 500-300 BC. The outer set of two ramparts are less grand and probably slightly later in date.

Community projects

The monumental scale of enclosures like the ones on the Caterthuns and Tap o' Noth demonstrates that a good deal of surplus labour was available in the Iron Age, and that there were people around with the authority to marshall that resource. Construction projects of this scale would have taken farmers off the land for some time, so these were clearly not communities struggling to meet their basic food needs. The farmers of the Scottish lowlands must have formed a strong and well-provisioned population.

Meeting places and fortifications

The stone fort on the White Caterthun would have provided a virtually impenetrable barrier to attackers. None of the other ramparts around either hill, however, are anything like as substantial. Even more strikingly, these earthen ramparts are punctured by numerous entrances, where timber gates would once have stood. The middle and outer groups of ramparts of the Brown Caterthun have at least nine. Entrances are the weakest point in any defensive structure, and nine seems a little over-generous for any fort. Rather than keeping people out, the multiple gateways seem to positively invite access from the valleys below. Perhaps these ramparts, as at Traprain and Eildon Hill, enclosed places of communal gathering, of religious or social, rather than military significance.

THE CHESTERS, DREM, EAST LOTHIAN (35)
HISTORIC SCOTLAND
NT 506 782

How to get there

Turn south from the B1377 just west of Drem. Within less than half-a-mile (1km) is a sign-post pointing out the pathway to the fort. There is no parking further down this track.

A show of strength

The Chesters gives the initial impression of invulnerability. Multiple high ramparts surround an inner area some 120m by 50m, and as many as five separate barriers would have guarded the entrances at either end (47). Inside are upwards of twenty circular house foundations, each the stance of a substantial timber building. Some appear to overlie parts of the ramparts, suggesting that the period of fortification was but one episode in the life of a settlement that was probably occupied from the middle of the first millennium BC until at least around AD 200.

Yet, while the leaky defences of the Brown and White Caterthuns might place in question the militaristic intent of their builders, it is difficult to beat the Chesters for sheer defensive incompetence. For only a literal stone's throw to the south is a much higher ridge than that on which the fort lies. From here one would have been afforded a fine view of the comings and goings within the walls, and the attacker would have been conveniently placed to shower the inhabitants with missiles of all kinds.

The Chesters fort was clearly built to impress, and actual defence seems scarcely to have been an issue in its design. Presumably no physical assault was anticipated. Instead it appears that the local leaders in this prime agricultural landscape of the East Lothian coastal plain had decided to devote the surplus labour, of what was a relatively well-off community, to the construction of an exceptionally grand, but ultimately rather pointless monument.

47 The Chesters, Drem, East Lothian, from the air; note the size of the fort relative to the farm buildings

RISPAIN CAMP, DUMFRIES AND GALLOWAY (36)
HISTORIC SCOTLAND
NX 429 399

How to get there

The track to Rispain Farm turns off the A746 less than half-a-mile
(1km) south of Whithorn. There is a car-park at the steading from which a short
sign-posted walk takes you to the site.

Variations on a theme

There are a great many regional variants of Iron Age fort in Scotland, and
Rispain is a good example of a fort radically unlike most of those described in
this chapter. While most tend to be circular or oval, Rispain is rectangular, and
was long thought to be either Roman or medieval in origin. A combination of
radiocarbon dates and artefacts have more recently placed its occupation in the
later centuries BC and the first couple of centuries AD.

The fort measures around 70m by 50m within a grassed-over double rampart
and ditch (originally about 6m deep), that would once have formed an impressive
barrier. The entrance lies at the north-east, where a wide causeway breaks the line
of the ditch. This entrance was originally marked by a large timber gate. From
here a metalled road ran towards the middle of the enclosure and a group of large
circular timber buildings. There is not a great deal to see inside, but a walk around
the rampart gives a good idea of how this seemingly low-lying site actually
occupied a dominant position over the surrounding landscape of rolling fields.

DREVA CRAIG, SCOTTISH BORDERS (37)
PRIVATE OWNERSHIP
NT 123 352

How to get there

The minor road running south-east from Broughton to Stobo passes over the
flanks of Dreva Hill. The fort of Dreva Craig lies immediately on the south side
of the road.

A boulder-strewn summit

Another intriguing little fort occupies the rocky peak of Dreva Craig, in the
Tweed Valley, standing dominant over a confined pocket of fertile ground
near the village of Broughton. Although never excavated, the surviving stone
foundations show something of the site's complexity (48).

The fort itself is not particularly unusual. Two thick boulder walls enclose a
stony summit no more than about 60m across. A walk across the interior reveals

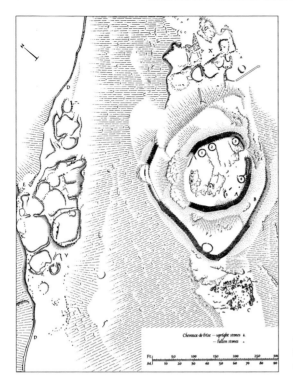

Chevaux-de-frise — upright stones ᴸ
— fallen stones .

48 A plan of the fort and adjoining settlements at Dreva Craig, Scottish Borders

the remains of at least five circular stone buildings, some at least built into rubble from the wall (and thus post-dating the fort proper). Downslope to the west lie the sprawling remnants of field banks and roundhouses which probably date a little later than the fort itself, perhaps to the early centuries AD. Some of these roundhouses measure around 8-10m across between their walls, and would have been quite impressive buildings when their walls stood to head-height and were capped with high conical roofs.

A shield of stones

What makes Dreva Craig of particular interest, however, is the rare survival, on its shallow southern approach, of a dense scatter of about one hundred jagged upright stones deliberately set into the ground. This is one of only a handful of known British examples of a type of defensive feature known as *chevaux-de-frise*. Many of the stones have been broken and many more are probably long gone, but it is extremely fortunate that any such handy building stones survive in their original positions at all. There may once have been more on the northern approach, but a later settlement of roundhouses has obliterated any traces.

Chevaux-de-frise represent one of the very few instances where one can suggest direct contact between the tribes of the Scottish Iron Age and their contemporaries in other parts of Europe. Timber *chevaux-de-frise*, formed of pointed stakes rather than stones, first appeared in Central Europe during the Later Bronze Age. Their purpose was to impede intruders, perhaps particularly to block cavalry attacks, but they would also have made for an impressive display. Stone versions have been identified in Iberia, Ireland and Wales, as well as Scotland (including one example in Shetland, at a site known as Burgi Geos). They may have been as much an exotic architectural flourish intended to provide a rather grand frontage to the fort, as a practical military device.

PITCUR, PERTHSHIRE AND KINROSS (38)
PRIVATE OWNERSHIP
NO 253 374

How to get there
Pitcur souterrain lies in a small fenced enclosure at the edge of an arable field on the north side of the A923, about 1¼ miles (2km) south-east of Coupar Angus. It is best approached from the south-west, along the edge of the field. You will need a torch to fully appreciate the still-roofed chamber.

Sunken chambers
While hillforts may be the most visible monuments of the Iron Age throughout most of south and east Scotland, they did not predominate everywhere. Far more common in the eastern lowlands, particularly north of the Tay, were souterrains (sometimes known as 'earth-houses'), one of the most characteristic but least understood types of Iron Age monument. These were sunken, stone-lined, curving passages, peculiarly similar to structures found in Brittany, Ireland and Cornwall.

Many souterrains were discovered towards the end of the nineteenth century, when increasingly zealous arable cultivation occasionally led to horse and plough disappearing through the roofing slabs of a previously unknown souterrain. The site at Pitcur, which was found and emptied around this time, is one of the best preserved and certainly the most complex souterrain to be seen anywhere in Scotland.

An Iron Age maze
Most souterrains are simple curving passages, with a narrow entrance at one end, and a wider, rounded stump at the other. Pitcur, however, is much more complicated, seemingly made up of at least two separate curving passages inter-linked by low, lintelled doorways. One of the passages retains most of its original roof; a rare survival for a prehistoric building.

Judging from the evidence of more recent excavations on other sites, the Pitcur souterrain would have been entered from a timber roundhouse (49). The remains of such a building probably still survive under the undulating mounds

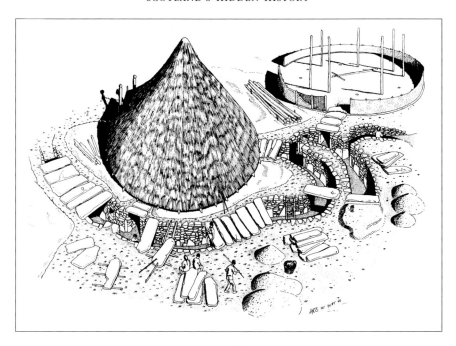

49 Artist's impression of a souterrain being built; based on Pitcur

between the passages (probably the debris of past excavations). It is ironic that the souterrain, sunken and inconspicuous during its lifetime, is now the only visible part of the settlement, while the great timber houses that would have most impressed the Iron Age visitor have entirely disappeared.

The earliest souterrains in Scotland seem to date from the last few centuries BC, while some, like Crichton (see below), cannot have been built before the second century AD. It is far from clear where the Pitcur souterrain fits into this spectrum. Fragments of a Roman bowl and a Roman coin were reputedly found during the nineteenth-century excavations, but all the finds have long since vanished. In any case, Roman finds may easily have been dumped along with other refuse into the roofless ruins of souterrains long after their construction and use.

Hidey-holes, temples or cellars?

The original purpose of souterrains has, unsurprisingly, been the subject of much speculation. It is unlikely that they were places of refuge (as was once thought), since their roofs would usually have been at or above ground level. Although their narrow entrances might have been easy to defend, a simple fire, the removal of a few roofing slabs, or a long enough wait, would presumably have been enough to winkle out any hapless defender.

Since souterrains seem almost purpose-built to hamper access, they were clearly not byres, and, although entered from houses, they show no traces of human habitation. Some may have been used for metal-working or other industrial functions once they had fallen into disrepair, but the lack of light and air would have ruled this out when they were roofed.

As with much in archaeology that defies easy explanation, it has been suggested that souterrains were ritual structures. Supporting evidence for this is limited, but might include the placing of cup-and-ring marked stones in certain parts of the souterrain walls. At Pitcur there are several stones bearing cup-and-ring markings, which were carved thousands of years before the souterrain was built. The most obvious now lies flat on the surface above the souterrain, but would once have been a capstone for the roof. Yet while there probably was some ritual dimension to these buildings, they were not seemingly dedicated religious buildings.

Perhaps most likely is the theory that the cool, dry conditions made them suitable for the storage of cereals and dairy produce. If true, this would suggest that very large quantities of food could be amassed by Iron Age communities in the east of Scotland even before the Roman invasion created a possible market for an agricultural surplus. Until experimental work is carried out on either a real or replica souterrain we will not be sure how likely this theory really is. At present, however, it seems to be the best we can come up with.

The implications of the storage theory are quite sobering when applied to Pitcur. If we imagine the mass of inter-weaving passages stacked from floor to capstones with grain, milk containers, meat and cheeses, it is difficult not to be impressed by the sheer productivity, wealth, and organisation of the local Iron Age population.

CULSH, ABERDEENSHIRE (39)
HISTORIC SCOTLAND
NJ 504 054

How to get there
Culsh souterrain sits in a fenced enclosure tucked against the south side of the A974 about 4½ miles (7km) north of Aboyne. A torch can be collected at the adjacent Culsh farm if you haven't brought your own.

A model souterrain
Unlike the sprawling tangle of the Pitcur souterrain, that at Culsh conforms closely to the typical plan of an elongated curving passage and is roughly 10m long by 2m wide. Entering from the south, you have to crouch and squeeze your way around the initial curve, before the passage widens and heightens to above head-height. The site is most remarkable, however, for the intact survival of its roof of massive flagstones.

ARDESTIE AND CARLUNGIE, ANGUS (40-1)
HISTORIC SCOTLAND
NO 502 344 (ARDESTIE) AND NO 511 359 (CARLUNGIE)

How to get there
These two sites, less than 1¼ miles (2km) apart, are each sign-posted from the A92 just east of Broughty Ferry. No torch required.

Souterrains in context
A little more idea of the original place of souterrains within Iron Age settlements can be gained from these two neighbouring sites in Angus, both of which were excavated around fifty years ago. Although neither is preserved to anything approaching roof height, both are worth a visit for their structural complexity (more than Culsh, less than Pitcur) and their traces of above-ground buildings.

The clearest traces are at Ardestie where the lower courses of at least four paved, stone-walled structures survive. These small buildings seem to have been used for metal-working. They probably represent only a fraction of the original settlement, but they do at least hint at what might lie beneath the surface around the open passages at Pitcur and elsewhere.

Souterrain landscapes
Ardestie and Carlungie are not unusual in their proximity. Indeed, the evidence of cropmarks shows that souterrains were densely spread across the eastern lowlands, particularly in Angus and Perthshire. This seems to suggest two things: firstly, that a considerable surplus of agricultural produce was being generated by the Iron Age farmers of lowland Scotland in the centuries prior to (and maybe during) the Roman invasion; and secondly that this surplus was stored by small communities and was not apparently commandeered by tribal chiefs or kings.

CRICHTON, MIDLOTHIAN (42)
PRIVATE OWNERSHIP
NT 400 619

How to get there
Crichton souterrain lies in a fenced enclosure in an arable field, on the south side of a minor road reached by turning right off the A68 south of Pathhead. The entrance can be a little slippery in wet weather. Remember to take a torch.

A buried chamber

Once through the cramped and awkward, but mercifully short, side entrance passage, this souterrain takes on the usual dimensions; roofed comfortably above head-height and about 2m wide (*50*).

The debris of Rome

The most extraordinary feature of the Crichton souterrain is the use in the walls of dressed stones apparently pillaged from an abandoned Roman installation or quarry (*51*). These are easily identifiable by their distinctive chisel marks. One stone, forming part of the roof, displays a carved Pegasus, the emblem of a Roman legion.

Most of this Roman material has been used either at doorways or other prominent areas, probably in order to convey some message regarding the status of the souterrain builders. Perhaps they aspired to Roman military proficiency, or maybe they saw themselves as conquerors of the Roman army and this stonework was their battle spoils. The use of all this Roman stonework provides rare proof that souterrains were still being constructed during or after the Roman period. Crichton probably dates to around the latter half of the second century AD or later.

50 Inside Crichton souterrain

CASTLELAW, MIDLOTHIAN (43)
HISTORIC SCOTLAND (THE ADJACENT FORT OF CASTLE KNOWE IS IN PRIVATE OWNERSHIP)
NT 229 638

How to get there

Castlelaw hillfort and souterrain occupies a knoll on the east side of the Pentland Hills, commanding wide views over the surrounding countryside. The site car-park, close to Castlelaw steading, is reached by a minor road sign-posted from the A702 a few miles south of the Edinburgh by-pass. The site itself is about 100m further uphill.

The ruined fort

At first glance Castlelaw seems a fairly typical hillfort: the multiple grassy ramparts surround a fairly small interior, with no obvious sign of internal buildings, although the prominence of the site within the landscape lends it a certain gravitas. Excavations, in the 1930s and 40s, revealed a complicated history, with an early palisaded work giving way first to a single rampart, and then to the multiple ramparts visible today (52).

Opposite: 51 This
photograph shows some
of the finely finished
Roman stonework
built into the walls of
Crichton souterrain

Right: 52 The fort of
Castlelaw, Midlothian,
seen against the backdrop
of the Pentland Hills.
The entrance to the
souterrain is visible in the
foreground of the fort

The hidden souterrain

What makes Castlelaw particularly unusual is that late in its occupation, once the
defences had been more or less abandoned, a massive souterrain, some 20m long
with a large round side-chamber, was built into one of the ditches.

Under the gaze of the ancestors

The other peculiar feature of Castlelaw is the presence, on the next summit, just
up the hill to the north-east, of an apparently earlier and rather smaller fort known
as Castle Knowe. This site is much less obvious than the fort below, but around
the northern approach you should be able to make out two shallow grooves,
about 6m apart. These are the remains of narrow trenches that would once have
held timber palisades, or stockades. A steep rocky slope to the south probably
rendered any defensive works there largely redundant, while to the north-east,
the palisade trenches seem to have been replaced by a bank and ditch for a short
stretch close to the entrance. The foundations of at least three roundhouses are
visible as slight platforms quarried into the slope inside the fort.

Without more modern excavation we cannot know exactly what the sequence
of events was on the hill, but it seems likely that the higher site was abandoned
to build the more impressive Castlelaw fort.

QUEEN'S VIEW, PERTHSHIRE AND KINROSS (44)
FORESTRY COMMISSION
NN 862 601

How to get there
The homestead at Queen's View is sign-posted as part of a Forest Enterprise trail on the north side of Loch Tummel. The quickest way to reach it is by following the forest track which heads uphill just east of the Queen's View visitor centre. A marked footpath branches off after around 100m and this leads up the short walk to the site.

Into the uplands
While open farming settlements with souterrains seem to have dominated the fertile lowlands of eastern Scotland, stone-built roundhouses known as homesteads seem to have been rather more common in the uplands. The Queen's View homestead lies in an exceptionally impressive location: despite the modern forestry plantation, the view from the entrance (clear of trees for the benefit of the electricity pylons!) looks straight down over Loch Tummel to Schiehallion.

Between north and south
The homestead was a sturdy stone roundhouse, about 17m in diameter within a stone wall about 3m wide. It was, in outward appearance, probably not unlike the broch towers of the north and west, of which we will see more in the next chapter, although its walls were solid, without chambers or stairs, and probably not particularly high.

Such buildings seem to have been roofed in much the same way as the northern broch towers and, for that matter, the southern timber roundhouses, with great conical, timber-framed, thatched roofs. It is easy to appreciate from inside the Queen's View homestead just how large and imposing a building this would have been, the apex of its roof perhaps 10m above the ground floor.

EDIN'S HALL, SCOTTISH BORDERS (45)
HISTORIC SCOTLAND
NT 772 603

How to get there
The site is sign-posted down a track to the south off the A6112. Cross the bridge at the bottom of the track and follow the signs across open ground along the side of the river. The walk takes at least twenty minutes.

A southern broch?

Even closer in appearance to the broch towers of the north and west is the stone roundhouse at Edin's Hall, which sits on the edge of a steep slope above the Whiteadder Water (53). The site is one of a scatter of so-called lowland brochs which are dotted around southern Scotland. But Edin's Hall is a complex site of which the broch forms just one part.

The broch sits within a hillfort, formed by two large ramparts and ditches, which is probably the earliest element of the site. Inside are squeezed the stone foundations of numerous slighter roundhouses, many of which were built into and over the ramparts which had by then begun to decay. The largest roundhouse, in the centre of the fort, is actually not much smaller than the broch in terms of its internal dimensions, and would originally have been a reasonably grand structure in its own right.

At the rear of the fort, and probably the last major building on the site, is the broch itself, still standing to around head-height (although it has been partly reconstructed). A porch and deep entrance passage, the latter flanked by cells on either side, gives access to a large, open central area. Within the thickness of the walls are a series of cells, with stairs leading to a now-vanished upper floor. This was clearly a massive, monumental building, with multi-storey accommodation. Architecturally it was closer to the broch towers of the north and west (see Chapter 6) than to most other buildings in this part of the country. The structure remains undated, but others like it in southern Scotland do not seem to have been built much before the first century AD.

53 Edin's Hall

Generations of display

The site as a whole seems to represent a series of stages in the aggrandisement of the inhabitants. First the fort, with its high ramparts and deep ditches, would have presented an impressive sight to the visitor. The big roundhouse in the centre, which probably post-dates the ramparts by a few centuries, would, in turn, have been a fine building by the standards of the day. Finally, the broch, with its scale and solidity, would have provided an unambiguous restatement of the power, connections and wealth of the inhabitants.

Iron Age miners

The source of this affluence may lie close by. As you walk towards the fort, crossing the bridge over the Whiteadder Water, you pass by a series of old copper mines. The copper deposits here were probably worked in the Iron Age, as they were in medieval times, and the control of this valuable resource may explain why a site of such unusual grandeur should occur in this particular place.

6

Broch towers
and the Atlantic zone

The Iron Age in the north and west of Scotland has a range of monuments that are quite distinct from those of the south and east (54). The tendency to build in stone, often on a monumental scale, has led to the remarkable survival of many of these buildings, in some cases right up to roof height.

Best known of all are the broch towers; elaborate architectural creations that display a mastery of drystone construction unmatched in Britain. Not surprisingly, these extraordinary buildings have attracted a vast amount of attention from antiquarians and archaeologists since interest in the prehistoric past first stirred over a century ago.

Debate has raged over the origins and function of brochs, with some seeing them as the products of invaders from the south of England or even further afield. Recent research, however, suggests that they evolved locally, in the last couple of centuries BC, from simpler stone roundhouses that can be traced back to around 600 BC, particularly in Orkney. Ultimately, like the timber roundhouses of the south and east, broch towers formed a regional variant (albeit a spectacular one) of the Iron Age roundhouse tradition that extended right across Britain, from Wessex to Shetland.

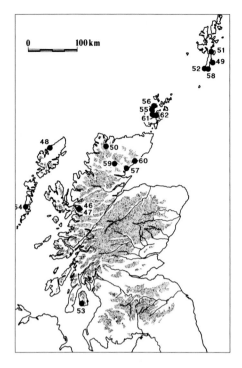

54 Map of sites in Chapter 6

DUN TELVE AND DUN TRODDAN, LOCHALSH, HIGHLAND (46-7)
HISTORIC SCOTLAND
NG 829 172 AND 834 172

How to get there

These two broch towers stand in the upper reaches of Glen Beag, reached by following the minor road which leads south from Glenelg. Dun Telve is reached first, while Dun Troddan lies a few hundred metres further east.

Twin towers

Glen Beag is remarkable in housing two of the four best-preserved broch towers in Scotland (the others being Mousa and Dun Carloway, below). Dun Telve, by the river on the floor of the glen, stands around 10m high (55), while Dun Troddan, perched on the rocky hillside, is only a little lower. Both have the thick wall bases (about 4.5m), characteristic of all brochs, which narrow as the walls rise, accentuating the visual impression of great height. Although, like so many well-preserved prehistoric structures, both were cleared out in the early years of the twentieth century, we can be tolerably confident that they were built between about 200 BC and AD 100.

Just why two such impressive buildings were built so close together in this seemingly remote glen remains a mystery. It may be that broch towers of this scale were fairly common around the north and west but survive here thanks to their seclusion, and the relative lack of subsequent stone-robbing. Or perhaps an uneasy relationship between the builders of these two neighbouring towers led them to try to outdo each other with the grandeur of their houses.

The shattered tower

Dun Telve, on the lower ground, is fronted by a clutter of what appear to be later stone buildings. As with all broch towers, only one narrow doorway at ground level punctures the outer shell of masonry. A corbelled cell opens from the right as you pass along the entrance passage. This was perhaps used for storage or accommodation, but is probably not, as was once thought, a 'guard cell' (anyone coming in could presumably block it with a shield). Nonetheless a bar-hole in the wall, behind the recess where the heavy wooden door would have been set, shows that some thought at least was given to security. The single, narrow entrance might have been easy to defend but it could just as easily have been blocked up or set alight by attackers. The timber roofs, too, would have been highly vulnerable to fire.

Once inside, the ragged edge of the surviving walls neatly demonstrates the principles involved in building a broch (55). At its most basic, the tower consisted of two concentric drystone walls, held together by rows of large flat slabs which form the floors and roofs of a series of superimposed galleries. You can see the remains of five of these galleries in the exposed wall section at Dun Telve.

The galleries are usually linked by stairs made from further large slabs. Access is provided via doors through the inner wall. At Dun Telve a door to your left as you enter leads into a small cell and staircase which would originally have led up to the first floor gallery. This hollow-wall construction enabled the weight of stone to be kept to a minimum.

Looking up at the inner wall-face you can see another characteristic feature of broch architecture. Just above head-height runs a projecting ledge known as a scarcement. Another can be seen much further up, almost 9m above the floor. These ledges seem to have been designed to support the timber first floor and probably, in the case of the upper scarcement, the roof.

Animal quarters

Dun Troddan, just along the glen, displays many of the same structural characteristics as its neighbour. It also, however, provides some clues as to how life in these broch towers may have been organised. Entering the structure today, you will encounter the remains of a series of post-holes and a hearth. These were found during the early excavations and are sometimes thought to represent the main domestic focus of the building (a broken quern-stone, for grinding grain, can also be seen built into the hearth).

However, if you look at the level of these features compared to the entrance, you will see that the floor is markedly uneven and that the post-holes and hearth

55 Dun Telve

seem to sit on a mound of earlier deposits, probably accumulated over many centuries. In fact, when first built, the ground floor of the broch tower may not have been occupied by people at all. The inner wall-face around the ground floor at Dun Troddan is poorly finished, in marked contrast to the walls above the scarcement ledge. This arrangement has led to the suggestion that it might have been at first floor level, on the long-vanished timber floor, that the broch-owning family lived, while the lower level was given over to stock and storage.

DUN CARLOWAY, LEWIS, WESTERN ISLES (48)
HISTORIC SCOTLAND
NB 189 412

How to get there
Dun Carloway (Carlabagh) is a prominent feature of the Lewis landscape, standing just south of the modern township of Carlabagh along the A858. The site is served by a small visitor centre and car park.

An Iron Age outpost
Despite the ravages of stone-robbing, Dun Carloway remains the tallest surviving broch tower in the Western Isles, standing to around 9m high (*colour plate 15*). It

is similar in many ways to Dun Telve and Dun Troddan, but it occupies a rather more imposing landscape setting.

Before entering, it is worth taking a walk around the foot of the outer wall (careful in wet weather). Round the slope from the entrance, the broch wall is skilfully moulded around the irregular rock outcrops of the hillside. Yet, despite this fine display of workmanship, one of the first things to strike the visitor entering the broch is the massive lump of natural rock which projects into the inner floor. This, like the stonework at Dun Troddan seems further evidence that the ground floors of these buildings were not the hub of the household.

Multi-storey living?

The cut-away reconstruction drawing (56) shows how Dun Carloway might once have been appeared. The stalling of stock on the ground floor would have provided extra warmth for the human inhabitants as well as shelter for the beasts themselves, much like the traditional byre-house dwellings of more recent centuries (and see also the reconstruction of a southern timber roundhouse in Chapter 5).

56 Dun Carloway, Lewis; artist's cut-away reconstruction

57 This interior view of Dun Carloway clearly shows the entrance to the gallery and, above it, the scarcement ledge which once supported the first floor. The two upper openings in the wall are 'voids' probably designed to let air and heat flow around the building

Counting floors

The reconstruction shows a full timber floor, the main living space, then a partially floored upper level and a large open space above it under the conical thatched roof. Much of this reconstruction (particularly the timber components) is guesswork of course, and it remains extremely difficult to estimate the number of potential floor levels in structures like Dun Carloway.

If we could simply equate the number of scarcement ledges to the number of floors then the ground floor at Dun Carloway would have been quite low and cramped while the first floor would have been open all the way up to the timber roof, with no upper floors of any kind (57). Although this might appear a little unlikely at first glance, we know that other stone roundhouses of similar date, known as wheelhouses (see Jarlshof, below) had only one floor, and that the distance from the floor to the apex of roof could sometimes be as much as 7m. This might tie in with the observation that the upper galleries of broch towers become very narrow and constrained and could not have been intended to give access. The uppermost galleries visible at Dun Carloway would always have been entirely impassable for an adult.

58 Mousa, Shetland; the best preserved of all brochs

MOUSA, SHETLAND (49)
HISTORIC SCOTLAND
HU 457 237

How to get there

This tallest and best-preserved of all broch towers stands on the coast of the island of Mousa facing across the channel to the east coast of mainland Shetland. The island is reached by ferry and it is a short walk south along the shore from the pier to the site. The chance to approach this site by boat gives a good feel of how early visitors must first have seen the great tower.

Tower of strength

It is at Mousa that one can gain the clearest impression of how the tallest broch towers would have appeared in their heyday (*58*). The massive, windowless shell of masonry broken only by a small, narrow doorway, rising and narrowing to its huge, conical roof would have made for an exceptionally imposing sight. Indeed, it remains a remarkably dominant feature in the landscape even today, clearly visible from the mainland for miles around.

Exploring the tower

Unlike Telve, Troddan or Carloway, the broch superstructure at Mousa is nearly complete. Walking along the dark galleries, up and down the stairs, and even standing in the central court entirely surrounded by the heavy cloak of masonry, you can gain a much deeper understanding of what it was like to inhabit these buildings. Mousa is also the only known broch tower where access is possible all the way to the wall-head which, at around 13m high, gives impressive views of the surrounding area.

Explaining the voids

Mousa is also the best place to consider another of the recurrent features of the best-preserved broch towers; the vertical rows of small openings, or voids, from the galleries to the interior, that rise from the first floor towards the wall-head. Mousa has four rows of voids, the function of which has never been conclusively established. It may be that they helped reduce the weight of stone above vulnerable lintels over the entrances to cells and galleries. Yet this explanation does not seem adequate to explain the creation of such seemingly weak points in the structure.

One recent study has suggested that the galleries in broch towers served mainly to insulate the inner wall from the worst of the weather and to maintain a flow of air around the building. In this model, the voids would have let the warm air from the hearth circulate in the galleries, keeping them dry and warm. This perhaps explains why so many upper galleries were built even when they were too narrow for access (not so of course at Mousa).

DUN DORNAIGIL, SUTHERLAND, HIGHLAND (50)
HISTORIC SCOTLAND
NC 457 450

How to get there

The broch tower stands in a fairly remote location by the Strathmore river just south of Alltnacaillich, about 15 miles (24km) south of Hope on the A838. It is impossible to miss it from the road.

A rubble-clogged reserve

Dun Dornaigil (or Dun Dornadilla) is another of the handful of brochs surviving to tower-like form (almost 7m high in this case), even if the high part of the wall is held up by a modern buttress (colour plate 16). Although much of the surviving super-structure is visible, the ground floor remains unexcavated and is thoroughly clogged with debris of its occupation and collapse. This is one of the few well-preserved broch towers to have escaped the attentions of the antiquarian's shovel and thus forms a most precious reserve of information.

The portal stone

Apart from its height, the most striking feature about Dun Dornaigil is the great triangular lintel which crowns its entrance. The shape of this huge stone probably helped divert the weight stresses from the superstructure away from the vulnerable entrance, but its visual impact would also have been important.

CLICKHIMIN, SHETLAND (MAINLAND) (51)
HISTORIC SCOTLAND
HU 464 408

How to get there

The site occupies an islet in a loch at the south end of Lerwick, now nearly surrounded by modern housing. Despite this, the sheer complexity and excellent preservation of the site makes it well worth a visit.

An islet broch

The broch tower at Clickhimin is an impressive structure in its own right, displaying many of the architectural features described above; including intramural galleries and stairs. The interior, however, is occupied by a later, smaller roundhouse, the walls of which mask the original inner broch walls.

59 This is an artist's impression of Clickhimin broch and blockhouse drawn in the 1960s. The roof would most probably have been conical and closed rather than open as shown here

Unlike the broch towers described so far, which have been more or less isolated structures, that at Clickhimin stands amid an array of subsidiary buildings, some earlier and some later than the main structure, and all set within a thick-walled enclosure (59).

Of particular importance is the imposing mass of stonework, known as the blockhouse, which fronts the enclosure, and which you pass through to reach the broch tower. Blockhouses are peculiar to Shetland, and share some architectural features with broch towers. The one at Clickhimin has a central passage with bar-holes which would have secured a wooden door. On either side are cells within the thickness of the wall, and along the inside edge runs a scarcement, suggesting the presence, at one time, of lean-to timber buildings. Although excavation suggested that the blockhouse may be a little earlier than the broch tower, the two appear to have co-existed for a time as part of one grand design.

The footprints of kings?

One other extraordinary feature of Clickhimin deserves mention. At the start of the causeway (by the modern gate) is a large flat slab bearing a carved footprint. Stones like this have been found at Dunadd, the traditional centre of the Scottish kings of Dalriada in Argyll, and in Ireland. They are generally thought to have been involved in the inauguration of kings. Whether the stone dates to the period of the broch tower or not, it does seem to imply that Clickhimin was once a site of considerable importance; perhaps the seat of Shetland's prehistoric kings?

NESS OF BURGI, SHETLAND (MAINLAND) (52)
HISTORIC SCOTLAND
HU 388 084

How to get there

Take the minor road along the Scatness peninsula as far as it goes. After that it is a walk of around half-a-mile (1km) to the site. The narrow causeway to the site is potentially treacherous in wet or windy weather (and this is Shetland).

A blockhouse settlement

Not all blockhouses are associated with broch towers. Indeed, the one at Ness of Burgi apparently forms the main focus of an Iron Age settlement. As at Clickhimin, this building is essentially a rectangular block of masonry, with a central entrance passage, cutting off the approach to the promontory (60). It sits behind a massive outer rampart and ditch, with a lower grassed-over rampart even further out (ignore the low stone cairn in between — it is debris from the excavation of the site).

60 Ness of Burgi,
Shetland, from the air

Blockhouses and brochs

The presence of well-built door checks and bar-holes, and of three formerly corbelled cells within the thickness of the walls, unequivocally link the site to the broch-building tradition. However, why some communities applied these architectural flourishes to roundhouses and others to blockhouses remains a mystery.

TORR A' CHAISTEAL, ARRAN, NORTH AYRSHIRE (53)
HISTORIC SCOTLAND
NR 921 232

How to get there

The track to this site is sign-posted from A841. The roundhouse lies on a ridge overlooking the sea, about 500m from the main road.

A restrained roundhouse

Although it is easy to be swayed by the grandeur of the broch towers, not all Atlantic roundhouses were so imposing. That at Torr a' Chaisteal is fairly small, around 14m in overall diameter, but, due to its thick walls, it is only around 7m in diameter inside. Not much survives of the actual masonry, although you can make out two courses around most of the circuit and an outer wall to the east. While it may have had an upper floor, Torr a' Chaisteal seems unlikely ever to have been a tower and is instead quite typical of many Iron Age homesteads along the west coast.

Iron Age farms

The sheer numbers of roundhouses in some islands, such as Barra and North Uist, are so great that they can never all have been homes to chiefs or kings. Instead they seem to have been the default settlement form for the land-holding classes; prosperous farmers rather than warrior lords. Torr a' Chaisteal seems to fit well into this picture, acting as a statement by its builders of their control over a modest patch of good farmland.

DUN VULAN, SOUTH UIST, WESTERN ISLES (54)
PRIVATE OWNERSHIP
NF 714 298

How to get there

The site occupies a spit of land between a sandy beach and a small loch on the west coast of South Uist. Turn west off the A865 at Bornish and follow the minor road to the beach.

A Hebridean homestead

Dun Vulan is a fairly well-preserved example of the generality of Atlantic roundhouses in the Western Isles, which had some architectural elaboration, such as cells or stairs in the walls, but which were probably never full-blown broch towers. The roundhouse itself is probably the earliest element of the site, dating to the last couple of centuries BC, while the accompanying open settlement spanned several subsequent centuries.

GURNESS, ORKNEY (MAINLAND) (55)
HISTORIC SCOTLAND
HY 381 268

How to get there

Take the minor road that branches off the A966 between Finstown and Birsay. The site is sign-posted and provided with a car-park.

A broch village

The broch of Gurness lies at the heart of a large stone-walled and multiple-ditched enclosure, now partly lost to the sea (61). Although the interior of this enclosure is densely packed with smaller houses, everything seems to

61 Gurness, Orkney, from the air

be focused on the broch. Entering through the main entrance, over the causeway through the walls and rock-cut ditches, the visitor is channelled along a formal path towards the door of the broch itself. Although perhaps not a tower like Mousa or Dun Carloway, this would have been a massive structure and the highly structured approach would have heightened the sense of its importance.

Inside the broch is a collection of stone fittings and furniture, including a large elaborately built well, not all of which are necessarily either contemporary or original to the construction of the building (*colour plate 17*). Nonetheless it gives some impression of the complexity of sub-division inside these structures that can be hard to recapture on other sites, where fittings were more commonly of timber, and have long-since rotted away. If the stone fittings are original then presumably Gurness, and many other Orcadian brochs, were quite different from the multi-storey byre-houses described above.

Society in stone

There were at least 20 broch villages in Orkney, with still more in Caithness, yet none approaches the order and symmetry of Gurness. Around the central building was laid out a series of cellular stone houses, each of near-identical design, as if to reinforce the social integration of the inhabitants, much as at Skara Brae thousands of years before (see Chapter 2). The scale, however, was rather greater, since Gurness could probably have housed some 30-40 families.

These broch villages were powerful statements of control, where the very architecture divided the inhabitants according to rank, with the head family settled comfortably in their broch at the physical as well as social centre of village life.

Kings of Orkney and beyond?

It seems clear that broch villages like the one at Gurness were centres of power, but how far did the power of their inhabitants extend? One extraordinary document from the classical world may provide some help. The historian Eutropius, writing in the fourth century AD, mentions that Orkney submitted to the Roman Emperor Claudius during his conquest of southern England in AD 43. Until recently, archaeologists have tended to dismiss this account, rather than accept the possibility that a king of Orkney could have taken such an active role in the affairs of the wider world, several decades before the Romans even reached southern Scotland.

Yet sherds of Roman amphorae (storage vessels which can be quite closely dated) found in the excavations at the site, suggest that someone at Gurness was apparently supping Roman liqueur wine at almost exactly this period, and certainly well before Agricola's troops marched into Scotland. It is tempting to speculate that the kings of Orkney had developed close links, perhaps through marriage or military alliance, with tribes far to the south, and were sufficiently up-to-date with the political situation in southern England to attempt to use it to their own advantage.

MIDHOWE, ROUSAY, ORKNEY (56)
HISTORIC SCOTLAND
HY 371 305

How to get there

Once on Rousay, head north-west along the B9064 for about 5 miles (8km), then follow the signs along the footpath down to the coast.

Across the water

On the coast, facing across the narrow strait that separates mainland Orkney from Rousay, stands the broch village of Midhowe. Like Gurness, it occupies a strongly built enclosure within a stout stone wall and rock-cut ditch. Although more compact in design it exhibits many of the same features, with particularly well-preserved internal fittings, and a cluster of subsidiary buildings crowding the surrounding enclosure.

A false start?

The internal stone furniture appears to relate to more than one period of occupation, and it is more than likely that, like any building occupied for any length of time, the broch was progressively modified. A particularly interesting feature here, however, is that the broch wall was built with a ground level gallery running right around the structure. This was later blocked up, and buttresses were added to the outside of the wall; seemingly the structure had become unstable and in need of more support at the base.

CARN LIATH, SUTHERLAND, HIGHLAND (57)
HISTORIC SCOTLAND
NC 870 013

How to get there
This site is easily visible from the modern A9 about 2½ miles (4km) north of Golspie. Follow the marked path from the car-park to the broch.

A mainland Gurness?
The broch at Carn Liath, like Gurness, occupies a stone-walled enclosure into which are crammed the foundations of innumerable houses. Although these are clearly of several different periods, some may well be contemporary with the broch, although the minimal records from the Victorian excavation of the site offer few clues. Despite the provision of an enclosure and formal entrance passage, access to the broch itself was strictly controlled, as the provision of elaborate door checks and a fine bar-hole at its entrance demonstrate.

JARLSHOF AND OLD SCATNESS, SHETLAND (MAINLAND) (58)
HISTORIC SCOTLAND (JARLSHOF), SHETLAND AMENITY TRUST (OLD SCATNESS)
HU 399 095, HU 390 106

How to get there
The settlement at Jarlshof lies close to the southern tip of mainland Shetland, next to the Sumburgh Hotel, and is reached via the A970. A small visitor centre houses artefacts and displays covering the lengthy occupation of the site. Old Scatnes is around 1.5km away to the north-east on the same road.

The 2000-year village
Jarlshof is a sprawling settlement containing remains of many periods, from the Later Bronze Age to the Viking period (the latter described in Chapter 9). At its core are the remains of a broch, half of which has long since fallen into the sea. But of most immediate interest here are a cluster of slightly later

wheelhouses; an entirely new structural form that seemingly originated in the last couple of centuries BC.

After the brochs

Wheelhouses are so-called because of their distinctive floor plan; the circular interior being divided up by a series of regularly-spaced radial piers (the spokes of the wheel). Wheelhouses have only ever been found in Shetland and the Western Isles, where they appear to have been slightly later in date than brochs (although their use probably overlapped). Oddly, despite over a century of intensive excavation, none has ever been found in Orkney.

At Jarlshof are the remains of at least three successive wheelhouses. The best preserved retains much of its roof; a series of corbelled bays surrounding an open central area that would itself have been capped by a conical thatched roof (62). Wheelhouses were masterpieces of drystone construction, their intricate roofing requiring arguably as much skill to produce as the more immediately impressive broch towers. In contrast to the broch towers, however, this skill could be appreciated only from inside the buildings. Perhaps there was now more social interaction taking place inside houses than there had been before.

Old Scatness

Just over 1 km north-east of Jarlshof recent excavations have exposed a strikingly similar but even better preserved broch complex at Old Scatness. Here a well-preserved broch tower is surrounded by a mass of later structures including

62 Artist's impression of life inside a wheelhouse

wheelhouses almost identical to those at Jarlshof. Using the most up-to-date analytical techniques, these excavations will in time add far more depth to our understanding of Iron Age life in Shetland.

ORD NORTH, SUTHERLAND, HIGHLAND (59)
PARTLY PRIVATE OWNERSHIP AND PARTLY FORESTRY COMMISSION
NC 574 055

How to get there
Head across the river from Lairg on the A839 and follow signs for the Ferrycroft Countryside Centre. An archaeological trail across the hillside starts from the Centre's car-park. Guide leaflets can also be obtained from the Centre.

Beyond the brochs
Not all of the survivals from the Atlantic Iron Age belong to the drystone building tradition of the brochs, blockhouses and wheelhouses. Equally common in some parts of the north and west are the remains of roundhouses built of stone and earth, and known as hut circles (*colour plate 14*).

The term hut-circle is a rather antiquated description of a type of monument found widely in the Scottish uplands, and particularly commonly in upland Perthshire and parts of the Highlands. Essentially these comprise ring-like banks formed by the collapsed turf and stone walls of prehistoric roundhouses. Usually the position of the entrance can be detected by a break in the bank. There are many variations on this simple form and it appears from the limited excavation evidence that houses of many periods, from before 1500 BC right through to the Roman period, may be represented.

A walk through time
The low hill known as the Ord, overlooking the southern end of Loch Shin, is littered with the remains of human settlement from the Neolithic period right through to post-medieval times. The sign-posted trail takes the modern visitor past two large chambered tombs close to the summit, many simpler Bronze Age burial cairns, and more than twenty hut circles.

Hut or house?
Without excavation it is impossible to give a date for the hut circles on the Ord, but it seems fair to assume that they cover a lengthy period of occupation. Although the term hut-circle suggests a rather cramped building, many of these structures would originally have been almost as imposing in appearance as the broch towers. Their floors were often larger than those of the broch towers, and reconstructions based on the few excavated examples produce impressive, high-roofed buildings.

It seems then that hut circles too could act as statements of power: their builders were certainly keen to create houses that would stand out and be seen. One hut circle, at the south end of the Ord trail (lying on the modern fence line), is surrounded by a deep ditch and bank, in a break from the normal rambling unenclosed settlement pattern. Perhaps this hints at the kind of aggrandisement of the house that we have already seen in the broch towers further north and west.

KILPHEDIR, SUTHERLAND, HIGHLAND (60)
PRIVATE OWNERSHIP
NC 991 194

How to get there
Follow the A897 up the Strath of Kildonan to the bridge over the Kilphedir burn and park in the quarry. The site lies about 400m uphill to the north-east. Although not visible from the road, the broch become prominent after a couple of hundred metres. There are numerous other enclosures and hut circles in the glen, many of them marked on the Ordnance Survey map.

The hilltop broch
Little detail can now be made out within the huge mass of collapsed masonry that covers the broch, but the surrounding ramparts and ditches are impressive in their own right, as is the site's location, on a prominent knoll (63).

Brochs and hut circles
About 300m west of the broch, and slightly downhill, is a group of three hut circles. One is a particularly thick-walled example which has a built-in souterrain (a somewhat smaller version of those discussed in Chapter 5) entered from below the house wall (although you should be mindful of the wet mud that accumulates within it). The lintelled roof of the souterrain is still in place for almost 10m of its length.

It is tempting to make a link between the spatial arrangements of structures like this hut circle, with its peripheral souterrain, and those of the broch towers with their encircling galleries. Excavations of some Kilphedir hut circles during the 1960s showed that a few may date to the last couple of centuries BC — about the same time as the broch towers.

Although they overlap in areas like Caithness and Sutherland, the main broch areas are distinct from the main hut circle concentrations. Did the more massively walled hut circles, with their added souterrains, perhaps develop in parallel with brochs, with the latter perhaps becoming dominant later on? Perhaps the broch at Kilphedir is a direct replacement for the hut circle and souterrain nearby. We are a long way from disentangling these relationships, but

63 The broch at Kilphedir, Sutherland, stands out on the hilltop. The hut circles occupy the high moorland around it

the superb preservation of prehistoric landscapes in the north and west at least holds out that possibility.

RENNIBISTER, ORKNEY (MAINLAND) (61)
HISTORIC SCOTLAND
HY 397 127

How to get there
Head west from Kirkwall along the A965 for about 4 miles (6.5km). A sign-post directs you into the car-park. Do not be tempted to park in the farmyard itself.

A sunken chamber
Souterrains are also found in the broch heartlands of Orkney, although they tend to be quite different from those in the south and east. The one at Rennibister Farm is entered nowadays via a ladder through a gap in the roof. This takes you into an oval chamber with a fine corbelled roof supported by four stone pillars. Originally, however, it would have been entered by crawling along a narrow entrance passage.

Rediscovering the dead
In many ways the Orkney souterrains bear an uncanny resemblance to the much earlier chambered tombs (see Chapter 3). The superficial similarity is heightened at Rennibister by the extraordinary discovery of the mingled bones of six adults

and twelve children on the floor of the chamber when it was first opened in the 1920s. This burial seems quite out of place in an Iron Age context, but it does provide a useful reminder of how little we know both about the various uses to which souterrains were put, and about the religious beliefs of Iron Age societies in general.

GRAIN, ORKNEY (MAINLAND) (62)
HISTORIC SCOTLAND
HY 442 117

How to get there
This souterrain lies in an industrial estate on the outskirts of Kirkwall. Follow the A965 westwards and turn right just after the harbour. The site is on Scott's Road, second on the right.

Absent houses
The Orkney souterrains are further distinguished from those of the south by being more or less entirely buried below ground. This is nowhere better exemplified than at Grain souterrain (*colour plate 18*), which lies under 2m of soil and, like Rennibister, consists of an oval chamber reached by a painfully low passage (somewhat heightened in recent times by digging into the rock floor). However, like their southern cousins, these buildings seem to have been associated with above-ground houses and cannot be viewed as hiding places or refuges.

1 Knap of Howar, Orkney

2 Eilean Domhnuill, North Uist

3 Skara Brae, Orkney

4 Stanydale, Shetland

5 The Grey Cairns of Camster, Caithness

6 Midhowe, Orkney

7 Inside the chamber at Maes Howe, Orkney

8 The Ring of Brodgar, Orkney

9 Callanish, Lewis

10 The Hill o' Many Stanes, Caithness

11 Cairnpapple, West Lothian

12 Traprain Law, East Lothian

13 The White Caterthun, Angus

14 Reconstruction of a hut circle settlement in Holyrood Park, Edinburgh

15 Dun Carloway, Lewis

16 Dun Dornaigil, Sutherland

17 Stone structures inside the Broch of Gurness, Orkney

18 Inside the souterrain at Grain, Orkney

19 Ardoch Roman fort, Perthshire

20 The Antonine Wall, Croy Hill, North Lanarkshire

Above: 21 Dunadd, Argyll

Left: 22 Pictish stone at
Aberlemno, Angus

23 Sueno's Stone, Moray

24 The Brough of Birsay, Orkney

25 Jarlshof, Shetland

7

The Roman interlude

After a generation or more of conquest and consolidation in southern Britain, the Roman army advanced into Scotland in AD 79. Its commander was Gnaeus Julius Agricola, governor of the Roman province of Britannia. The aim was to complete the Roman conquest of the whole island of Britain. This, however, was never to be achieved. Instead the Roman encounter with Scotland was to comprise more than a century of sporadic military action and abortive attempts at occupation, before the army finally gave up its attempt to absorb the north within the Empire (64).

A combination of historical and archaeological evidence points to three main periods of conflict. The first started with the Agricolan invasion in the reign of the Emperor Vespasian; the first of the Flavian dynasty. A biography of Agricola by his son-in-law Tacitus provides an invaluable outline of the events surrounding the conquest. After routing the combined forces of the indigenous tribes at the Battle of Mons Graupius, and pounding coastal communities as far north as Orkney with his fleet, Agricola began to strengthen his grip. A network of garrison forts and smaller installations held the south and east of the country in a virtual stranglehold. Yet the Flavian occupation ended abruptly in the late AD 80s, when an imperial change of heart withdrew the army south to the line later followed by Hadrian's Wall in modern Northumberland and Cumberland.

The second occupation began in the AD 140s when the Emperor Antoninus Pius ordered a new assault on Scotland. It is this Antonine occupation that has left the most durable physical traces; most notably of course the Antonine Wall, which marked the formal northern limit of the enlarged Empire. Again, however, the stay was fairly brief, and by around AD 165 the army had withdrawn once again to the old line on Hadrian's Wall.

64 Map of sites in Chapter 7

Then again, in the first decade of the third century AD, the Emperor Septimius Severus and his sons Geta and Caracalla, launched the final full-scale assault by land and sea. The campaign was brief, however, and effectively ended with the death of the Emperor in York in AD 211. Thereafter contact was limited to periodic raids by both sides, never resulting in lasting conquest.

BURNSWARK HILL, DUMFRIES AND GALLOWAY (63)
PRIVATE OWNERSHIP
NY 186 787

How to get there
Take the B725 east of Ecclefechan, turning left onto a minor road after the railway bridge. After about 1½ miles (2.5km) the road passes through a patch of woodland, then emerges on the southern flank of Burnswark Hill. The southern of the two Roman camps is then immediately on your left. Allow a few hours if you intend to explore all the various features.

A south-western centre

The looming presence of Burnswark Hill forms a major landmark in Annandale, and like Eildon Hill North and Traprain Law, the hill would always have been an eminently suitable location for a prehistoric power centre. It is perhaps not surprising then that the summit is enclosed by a system of ramparts forming a defended stronghold some 17 acres (7ha) in extent; presumably a major Iron Age centre. As well as these ramparts, a burial cairn on the summit, and evidence of Neolithic and Bronze Age activity found during excavation, hint at a lengthy period of occupation and use. Further Iron Age enclosed settlements lie on the slopes east and west of the fort.

Roman and native

Below the amorphous linear mound formed by the tumbled remains of the rampart, excavation revealed twin lines of large post-holes. The timbers that once stood in these sockets would have supported a barrier much more formidable than the denuded remains might otherwise evoke. The remains of house stances (not obvious on the surface, but proven by excavation) suggest that up to around 150 timber roundhouses may have occupied the limited habitable areas of the hilltop during the first millennium BC.

The most intriguing feature of the site, however, is the presence on the north and south flanks of the hill of the substantial remains of two Roman camps (65). Together the camps encompass an even larger area of ground than the native enclosure. The northern camp is remarkably straggling and irregular by Roman standards. Roman military installations usually maintain a reasonably strict adherence to their conventional 'playing-card' shape, i.e. an oblong with rounded corners.

The southern camp overlies the remains of a still-earlier fortlet, showing that the camps were not the immediate product of the first Roman encounter with the tribes of southern Scotland. It is more conventional in shape than its northern neighbour, but retains evidence of a quite extraordinary feature. For along the side facing the hillfort lie three great artillery platforms, from which siege engines would have rained down missiles on the native defences just over 100m away.

Celts under siege?

In the absence of a known historical context for such a conflict in this part of Scotland, and given the likely early date of the native fortifications (probably built around 600 BC), it is usually thought that these Roman structures represent the remains of training camps, used to prepare troops for combat. Excavations have recovered plentiful evidence of stone balls fired from Roman ballistae, and lead sling-bolts, but these seem to have fallen not on huddled ranks of desperate defenders, but harmlessly onto the long-abandoned ruins of aged and decaying banks and ditches.

65 This aerial view shows one of the Roman camps on the flank of Burnswark Hill. The platforms for the Roman artillery are clearly visible on the right of the camp, and the earlier fortlet can be seen tucked into the bottom right corner

Nonetheless, despite the poor state of the defences at this time, excavations did show evidence of some native settlement just prior to the likely date of the camps in the mid-second century AD. It remains possible that humbled local worthies were ushered out of the settlement before the pounding of Roman artillery reinforced the subjugation of what may have remained a powerful symbolic location.

ARDOCH, PERTHSHIRE (64)
PRIVATE OWNERSHIP (PART OF THE CAMPS ARE IN THE CARE OF HISTORIC SCOTLAND)
NN 840 100

How to get there

Park at the north end of the village of Braco, then walk north across the bridge. The site is sign-posted through a gate in the wall on your right. Once through the gate you are immediately upon the defences of the fort.

A frontier fort

The fort at Ardoch is one of the best preserved Roman military sites in Scotland, occupying a strategically important position around 15 miles (25km) (or one day's march) north of the Antonine Wall (*colour plate 19*). It seems to have been known to the Romans as Alauna on the basis of references in the work of the geographer Ptolemy about AD 140.

Cosmopolitan forces

Ardoch bears traces of all three major Roman incursions into Scotland. The first fort was built during the early 80s AD, to house part of the Roman garrison after the victory at Mons Graupius. A tombstone dating to this period records a soldier of cohors I Hispanorum, a Spanish regiment of some 500 infantry and cavalry who were stationed here at that time. It is not always appreciated that the majority of those serving in the Roman army were not from Italy, far less Rome itself. Even recently absorbed Celtic tribesmen from what is now England and Wales probably fought for Agricola.

A change of mind

After only a few years of occupation, a change in Imperial policy resulted in the withdrawal of Roman troops from Scotland. Ardoch, like many other installations, was abandoned. In the Antonine period, however, about AD 140, the northern frontier was pushed forward once again, and many new forts were built on old sites which had retained their strategic importance.

Ardoch was now one of several forts which served as outposts to the north of the Antonine Wall. The defences visible today are dominated by those of the final phase of modification around AD 158. Yet again, however, this inclusion of southern Scotland within the empire was to prove abortive, and the fort was finally abandoned about AD 163, when the Roman forces were pulled back to the line of Hadrian's Wall.

Although the fort itself was never apparently re-occupied, the temporary camps which stretch to the north and west of the main installation include the remains of two enormous marching camps probably dating to the campaigns of Septimius Severus and his sons at the beginning of the third century AD.

Within the ramparts

As you enter the site today you cross the multiple ditches of the south-west corner of the Antonine fort. The interior is largely featureless, except for the foundations of a medieval hospice, but excavations at the end of the nineteenth century revealed rows of timber barrack blocks and other military buildings. Only one barrack block was of stone construction. It is worth noting the sheer scale of the interior, which occupies around 5 acres (2ha), and would have housed a strong military presence.

The most spectacular feature of the Ardoch complex, however, is the array of ramparts, banks and ditches, seen at their best on the east side, directly across the interior of the fort from the modern entrance. At this point there are 5 ditches with accompanying banks of earth and turf outside the inner rampart. A clearly-defined causeway gives access to the entrance, which would have been flanked by substantial timber gates, defended by high towers. The visible defences subsume the remains of an earlier phase of the fort: part of its surrounding rampart survives in the middle of the northern set of banks and ditches.

The preservation of these defences is truly exceptional, making Ardoch among the most impressive of Roman military remains in northern and western Europe. At its height, during the Antonine occupation, it must have been a highly effective symbol of Roman military might and the futility of resistance.

Beyond the fort

Exiting through the northern defences you enter what would have been the extensive annexe of the Antonine fort. This covers a huge area, much larger than the fort itself, extending all the way to the modern road which cuts across the site almost 400m to the north. The rampart which surrounded this annexe was no mean construction itself, and can still be followed along its west side where it hugs the edge of the modern road.

Although annexes are not uncommon on Scottish forts, few have been excavated and their function is not entirely certain. While some may have held civilian settlement, the one at Ardoch probably served a range of functions for the military garrison: it may have contained ovens, workshops, religious shrines etc.

An expanse of camps

Although a detailed survey of the fort was made by General William Roy as early as 1793, the full extent of the site was only discovered in recent decades when a series of overlapping temporary camps were observed on aerial photographs. As you stand at the northern limit of the annexe, looking to the north and west, you see only undulating arable fields. Yet under these lie the remains of the banks and ditches of camps which housed troops from several military campaigns, stretching around 1½ miles (2.5km) into the distance.

Camps such as these were built by the soldiers themselves for protection while they camped in hostile territory. The paths of individual campaigns can sometimes be traced by the trail of camps built and quickly abandoned as the army moved. These temporary enclosures were defended by a single ditch and inner rampart topped by palisade stakes. As they were usually occupied for only a short time, they generally contain fewer artefacts or internal structures than the forts, although excavations of camp interiors can reveal cooking areas, ovens and refuse pits.

Remnant camps

If you walk to the far north rampart of the annexe you will see (just before you get to the modern road) a parallel bank. This is part of one of the largest marching camps, dating to the campaigns of Severus in the early third century. The interior of this camp is more than 25 times greater than that of the fort. When in occupation, it would have been crowded with the tents and cooking fires of the huge Severan army. This gives some idea of the scale of the Severan invasion; the last attempt at the conquest of northern Britain.

The clearest surface trace of these camps lies some distance north of the fort. To reach it, carry on along the road north of Braco and turn left at the first junction. The site is immediately on your right and there is an interpretation board to show you are in the right place.

ARDUNIE, PERTHSHIRE (65)
HISTORIC SCOTLAND
NN 946 187

How to get there
Follow the minor road from Trinity Gask to Madderty. Park when you reach a 90° bend in the road about ½ mile (1km) north of Trinity Gask. If you then walk back westwards along the forest track for around ¾ mile (1.3km) you will reach the watch-tower immediately on your left. The forest track follows the line of the Roman road.

The edge of the Empire
Between Ardoch and the fort of Bertha, near modern Perth, to the north west ran a new road, established by Agricola's army. The road was guarded by a series of watch-towers set between ½ mile (0.8km) and 1mile (1.5km) apart, depending on visibility along the line. This road cut across the prominent Gask Ridge, parallel to the north of the modern A9, which would have given extensive views over the movement of people in Strathearn and the surrounding area. The original views from the ridge are rather obscured now by dense modern forestry plantations, which block off much of the intended open outlook, but you can catch glimpses of the wider landscape as you travel along the minor roads along the ridge.

Together, these forts, watch-towers and road formed the formal limit of the Roman Empire in the AD 80s; the Gask frontier. Indeed, not only was this the most northerly fixed frontier of the Roman empire, but, along with a similar system of roads and towers along the Rhine it was probably the earliest; an ancestor, at least in conceptual terms, of both Hadrian's Wall and the Antonine Wall.

With these towers in place it would have been impossible to cross the frontier unnoticed. Travellers would have had to report to the appropriate officials and pay the appropriate dues before they could traverse, unarmed and escorted from the wilds of Caledonia to the Roman province of Britannia.

A tower in the trees
One of the best preserved of the watch-towers can be seen at Ardunie on the Gask Ridge. The most visible feature today is the sizeable ditch with its rather less imposing internal bank. A single causeway leads into the tiny interior, a mere 12m in diameter.

Much of this meagre internal space would have been occupied by a tall timber tower, just under 4m along each side, resting on four massive upright posts. The post-holes for such constructions have been found without fail whenever these tower sites have been excavated. Our best evidence for their original appearance comes from the only marginally later scenes depicted on Trajan's Column in Rome itself. This majestic piece of self-congratulatory sculpture depicts similar two-storey towers constructed during the wars with Dacia, now part of the Balkans (*66*).

An unpopular billet

These towers would have been manned by small detachments, of only a handful of men, drawn from the larger garrisons of nearby forts. Their task was to deter and report trouble, rather than to stamp it out. It is easy to imagine the bleak conditions for the tiny garrison on this wind-blasted open ridge, on the edge of hostile territory, thousands of miles distant from the Mediterranean heartlands of the Empire. Nonetheless, their very physical presence and the imposition of these lofty towers along the horizon, would have had an important psychological effect in emphasising the presence of the army and in discouraging any thought of revolt.

The Gask frontier was destined to be short-lived, however, and seems not have lasted beyond the withdrawal of Agricola's army from Scotland towards the end of the AD 80s. Nonetheless, recent excavations of some Gask towers, including one just north of Ardoch, suggest that some of the towers went through a complex process of construction, repair and replacement, even within their brief term of occupation.

66 Artist's impression of the Roman watch-tower at Ardunie, Perthshire

MUIR O' FAULD, PERTHSHIRE (66)
HISTORIC SCOTLAND
NN 981 189

How to get there

Follow the minor road from Trinity Gask to Findo Gask. Park when you reach a 90° bend in the road about 1¼ miles (2km) east of Trinity Gask. Walking westwards along the forest track for around 300m you will reach the watch-tower immediately on your left. As at Ardunie, the forest track follows the line of the Roman road.

A stroll along the frontier

Muir o' Fauld lies three towers further along the Gask line from Ardunie, and is worth taking in on the same trip. A visit to both gives an impression of the standardisation of design in these constructions. Both would have stood at the same time and each would have had a similar garrison. At Muir o' Fauld, however, it is easier to see the remains of the outer bank which gave some added depth to the defences.

DURISDEER, DUMFRIES AND GALLOWAY (67)
PRIVATE OWNERSHIP
NS 902 048

How to get there

A track from the north end of the village of Durisdeer leads to the site some 1 mile (1.5km) distant.

Guarding the pass

Intermediate in size between full-scale forts and smaller installations such as watch-towers, were fortlets, miniature forts designed to hold a detachment of probably no more than 80 soldiers. One of the best preserved fortlets in Scotland is located in a spectacular location overlooking the Roman road as it climbs out of Nithsdale (67). It seems to date to the Antonine occupation, a couple of generations later than the Gask frontier.

A single rampart, some 9m thick, and a rock-cut outer ditch, surround an area just over 20m across. The entrance is positioned on the north-eastern side where it is afforded extra protection by an outer stretch of bank. Excavations in the 1930s showed that the timber barracks inside had been rebuilt on at least one occasion.

67 Durisdeer, Dumfries and Galloway, from the air

BIRRENS, DUMFRIES AND GALLOWAY (68)
PRIVATE OWNERSHIP
NY 218 752

How to get there
Follow the B722 west of Eaglesfield. The road soon turns to the north and after about
1 km the ramparts of the fort of Birrens appear on the left hand side of the road.

A garrison fort
The source of troops for the garrison at Durisdeer and other small installations
in the area was probably the major fort at Birrens, known to the Romans as
Blatobulgium. Whereas Ardoch was, at one point in its history, an outpost fort for
the Antonine frontier, Birrens served as an outpost for Hadrian's Wall on the road
north to western Scotland. It was built in the AD 120s on the site of an earlier fortlet,
rebuilt and enlarged in the AD 150s, and finally abandoned around AD 180.

The importance of this location to the Roman army is shown by the
clustering of temporary camps around it. Intensive campaigns of excavation in
the late nineteenth century, the 1930s, and again in the 1960s, make this one
of the better understood Roman forts in Scotland, and have produced many
artefacts and carved stones.

Nothing of the numerous internal buildings survives above-ground today, but the defences at the northern gate are well preserved and worth a visit. As at Ardoch a series of deep undulations marks the position of six ditches, flanking a causeway into the fort. The inner rampart survives as a low bank. The southern defences have been eroded away by the Mein Water.

DERE ST, SOUTRA, SCOTTISH BORDERS (69)
HISTORIC SCOTLAND
NT 464 567

How to get there
Heading south along the A68, take the B6368 to your right just past Soutra Farm. The medieval Soutra Aisle soon becomes visible on your left. The visible section of Roman road begins around 300m due south of the medieval building.

Containing the country
It is in the Roman period that Scotland, or at the least the southern part of the country, was treated for the first time as a geographical whole, and carved up accordingly with an integrated system of military installations and roads. The road along the Gask frontier was one early part of this system, but a better preserved road forms part of Dere Street, the main arterial line from the forts of northern England, through the Cheviots, to the Forth.

The communications revolution
Roman roads, bearing a dead straight course across the irregular landscape, are one of the clichés of popular history. Yet, while not as unflinching in their linear progress as popular imagination holds, they were indeed one of the prime achievements of the Roman military machine. Well-built metalled roads following the main natural and established communications routes across the countryside enabled the Roman army to move over land with what must have seemed near miraculous speed, and reduced the need for large and expensive garrisons in every potential trouble-spot. A not dissimilar strategy enabled the final subjugation of the Highlands by General Wade in the aftermath of the 1715 Jacobite Rising.

A line of attack
Dere Street was built to aid the progress of the Roman army during the first century AD. It lies for much of its length under the modern A68 (as in many cases, the line taken by the Roman army has not been bettered by more recent road-builders). The section at Soutra, however, has been left high and dry on the southern slopes of the hill, west of the modern road.

The main body of the road is clearly visible as a linear mound some 6m wide. Parts have been terraced into the hill-slope, the excavated material being redeposited to form the base of the road. The remains of partially silted-up pits along its western side are the last remnants of the small quarries which provided construction materials. Some stone would have been used, however, for kerbing and metalling.

Roads through history

Once built, roads were not easily removed, and long after the abandonment of any Roman hopes of conquest in the north, native armies of Picts and Scots would have taken advantage of these well-drained and durable route-ways to launch assaults deep into the heart of Roman Britain. The remains of a twelfth-century hospital and seventeenth-century burial vault (Soutra Aisle), close to this visible section of Dere Street, testify to the durability of the road as a communications link long after the collapse of the Roman province.

BAR HILL, EAST DUNBARTONSHIRE (70)
HISTORIC SCOTLAND
NS 708 758 (FORT)

How to get there

The path to the hilltop is sign-posted to the east of Twechar.

A new frontier

Of all the Roman monuments in Scotland the Antonine Wall is without doubt the best known. After several decades when the northern frontier of the Empire had been fixed on the line of Hadrian's Wall, south of the modern Anglo-Scottish border, the Antonine Wall represented a new extension of Roman sovereignty, reclaiming lands conquered but never consolidated by Agricola.

This new frontier, built in early AD 140s, comprised a massive turf-built curtain drawn across the narrowest part of Scotland, between the Firths of the Forth and Clyde. The Wall was reinforced by a line of attached forts, and its defensive qualities were further bolstered by a series of fortlets and smaller installations. Additional forts (including the refurbished Ardoch) ran north from the Wall as far as Bertha on the Tay. This Antonine network was apparently maintained until the army withdrew to Hadrian's Wall, around AD 165.

The lost wall

Unlike Hadrian's Wall, which is built largely of stone, the Antonine Wall seldom survives to any great height. Its fabric, mostly turf on a stone base, and occasionally earth and clay, has long since slumped and eroded to fill its accompanying ditch and obscure its original dimensions. Running, as it does, across the bustling core of Scotland's central belt, many sections have unsurprisingly disappeared under housing estates, quarries, or industrial complexes.

East of Glasgow, however, a lengthy stretch survives in reasonably good condition where it climbs over Bar Hill and Croy Hill; the highest points along its whole 31-mile (50km) length. Both sections also incorporate other Roman and native structures which are elsewhere often preserved only below ground.

The mechanics of the barrier

The line of the rampart and ditch which formed the principal components of the Wall are clear as you climb Bar Hill. Originally this rampart would have stood well over head-height, to around 3-4m high, with a timber stockade perched on the top. In front was a level area (known as the berm), before reaching the ditch, up to 4m deep and up to 12m wide, with a gentler bank of upcast material beyond. This great linear barrier was punctured only by the stout timber gates of the forts and fortlets. Behind, a broad and well-maintained road, known as the Military Way, running the length of the Wall, carried troops and provisions to wherever they were needed.

In all, this was a formidable barrier which would have occasioned a complete dislocation of the earlier landscape. For the indigenous peoples of the area it must have seemed an almost impossibly huge construction, preventing any unsupervised movement to the south and virtually sealing off the land annexed by Rome. Earlier native boundaries had existed, particularly in the form of linear earthworks seemingly denoting the limits of large land-holdings. Nothing north of Hadrian's Wall, however, could have prepared the local people for this extraordinary new construction. Only by assembling a substantial and determined military force could those living to the north ever hope to cross this boundary without sanction.

As you approach the summit of Bar Hill, you will come upon the remains of one of the Antonine Wall forts (68). This was set back around 30m from the Wall itself, but was probably constructed at much the same time. The headquarters building and the bath-house, with its well, have been excavated and left open to view. Just over 100m further on the Wall swerves slightly to the north around the faint remains of an earlier native fort, although it overlies its outer defences.

A land divided

Walking east along the line of the Wall it is easy to imagine the scene that would have met the Roman army patrols. To the left would have lain the broad boggy expanse of ill-drained lowland around the River Kelvin; probably sparsely populated and used mainly for grazing. Beyond, there would have been more arable farming and settlement on the rising slopes of the Campsie Fells, before the land rose again to the rough grazing lands of the higher peaks to the north. The

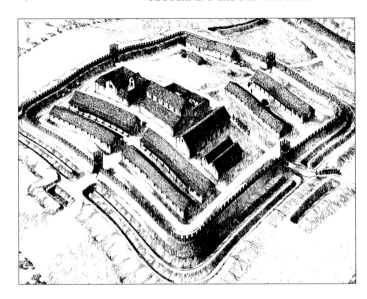

68 Artist's
impression of
the Roman fort
at Bar Hill

inhabitants of this area may have been seen as potentially threatening, outwith the
bounds of strict Roman control, but they were cowed by the regular supervision
of military patrols and the presence of outpost forts and the Wall itself.

To the right lay lands which now formed the most northerly part of an Empire
which stretched southwards as far as the Mediterranean, and beyond to North
Africa. Ahead and behind, the unbroken Wall struck out across the landscape to
the horizon and beyond.

CROY HILL, NORTH LANARKSHIRE (71)
HISTORIC SCOTLAND
NS 725 762 (WEST END OF STRETCH)

How to get there
This stretch of the Roman frontier lies a little to the east of Bar Hill. The path
is sign-posted from the north-west end of the village of Croy.

The next fort in line
As at Bar Hill, sections of the rampart and ditch can be followed across Croy Hill,
and the site of another fort can be visited on the east flank of the hill, below the
summit. The huge quarry to the south gives some idea of the pressures which
have led to the disappearance of so much of this massive but fragile monument.

As you climb this section of the Wall (*colour plate 20*), just as you leave the
last houses of the village behind, you can discern the remains of two low
platforms attached to the back of the rampart. These puzzling structures, known

as expansions, are found sporadically along the frontier, and are thought to have served as beacon stances, although this interpretation does not adequately account for their topographical location or (in this case) their proximity. Much as we know about this grand northern frontier, there is still much to learn (*69*).

ROUGH CASTLE, FALKIRK (72)
HISTORIC SCOTLAND
NS 843 798

How to get there
Follow the signposts from Bonnybridge towards Bonnyside Farm and keep going along the rather rough track to the car-park.

The Wall walk
If you walk west from the car park you can follow perhaps the best-preserved section of the Antonine Wall. The rampart and ditch are clearly visible, dotted with trees, for a few hundred metres. The modern track overlies the original Military Way, and between this and the rampart you can see the remains of quarry pits for the latter. Just beyond the cattle-grid you can also make out the remains of an expansion (see Croy Hill, above).

Ruins of a Wall fort
To the east of the car-park, across the burn, are the remains of the small fort of Rough Castle and its annexe, beyond. The fort is physically attached to the

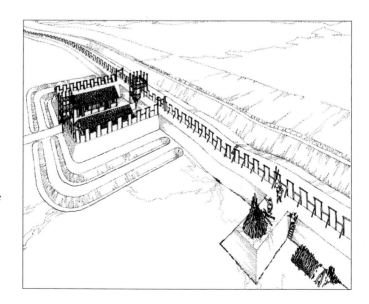

69 The Antonine Wall at Croy Hill; an artist's impression showing the fortlet and expansion

Antonine Wall, which forms its northern rampart. Although excavations revealed the presence of numerous closely-packed buildings, many built of stone, the interior is largely featureless today. Still visible, however, are the deep ditches that protected the buildings, particularly on the west side as you climb up to the fort from the bridge across the burn.

Gateway to the Empire

Crossing the interior and heading for the original north entrance, you will see the broad causeway which gave access from the fort out across the ditch. Here you are looking out from the limits of the Empire into Caledonia. It is here that traffic from the north would have crossed the border; Roman patrols and garrisons heading to and from the forts further north, as well as native farmers and merchants, conducting their daily business under the watchful eye of the garrison troops.

Across the causeway, the approach is flanked on the left by rows of small, close set pits. These are a defensive formation known as lilia, found during excavations in the early part of the century (*70*). Originally they would have contained sharpened stakes, and would have provided a virtually impenetrable barrier.

70 The close-set pits, or lilia, at Rough Castle, Falkirk, during excavation in 1904-5

71 The Antonine Wall at Watling Lodge

WATLING LODGE, FALKIRK (73)
HISTORIC SCOTLAND
NS 863 798

How to get there
Follow the signs from Bonnybridge. The remains of the Antonine Wall run along side the road immediately after the modern house of Watling Lodge.

A deep divide
This site is worth a visit just to appreciate the sheer scale of the frontier works (*71*). The ditch survives here to nearly its full depth of 4.5m and around 12m across, overlooking a steep drop to the north. The rampart, however, is not visible above ground.

SEABEGS WOOD, FALKIRK (74)
HISTORIC SCOTLAND
NS 818 792

How to get there
This stretch of the Antonine Wall runs parallel to the Forth and Clyde Canal, around 1 mile (1.5km) outside Bonnybridge on the Castlecary Road (sign-posted).

Fragments of a road

The remains of the rampart and ditch can be followed as they run across the scrubland known as Seabegs Wood. This part of the frontier is most notable, however, as the best preserved part of the Military Way, which runs parallel to the Wall, around 40m back from the rampart.

The Military Way appears as a low, but distinctly cambered mound around 7m wide. The large stones that made up the road's foundation have been exposed by several drainage channels. Originally this road would have run along the whole length of the Wall.

BEARSDEN BATH-HOUSE, EAST DUNBARTONSHIRE (75)
HISTORIC SCOTLAND
NS 546 720

How to get there

This site lies, conveniently, in Roman Road, Bearsden, and is sign-posted from the A809. The best place to park is at the public car-park about 250m west of the site.

A lost fort

The Roman fort which now lies substantially buried below the houses of Bearsden was originally, like Rough Castle, attached to the rear of the Antonine Wall. It probably measured just over 2½ acres (1ha) in extent with an annexe around half as big. None of this, however, is visible now. What does remain, within the annexe, is a splendid bath-house excavated during the 1970s and now laid out with explanatory boards (72). Among the finds from the excavations was the stone head of a goddess, thought to be Fortuna who protected the vulnerable bathers from the evil eye (73).

Cleanliness and empire

Bath-houses were a part of the ritual of life throughout the Roman Empire. Bathing was one obvious cultural characteristic which distinguished Roman soldiers in their own eyes from the barbarians around them. The bath-house at Bearsden would have been open to all the soldiers based at the fort.

The bath-house was a combined timber and stone construction; the stone elements being designed to prevent the risk of fire. The stone foundations have been left in place and the timber posts marked by modern stumps. Beside the bath-house is another import from the Empire; the latrine. This could have accommodated several soldiers at once: the timber seating over the main drain no longer exists. The latrine was flushed by water from the bath-house, through the rampart of the annexe, and into the ditch beyond.

72 Bearsden bath-house

Through the baths

The bath-house is best explored from west to east, entering from the west as Roman bathers would have done. At the west end are the remains of a timber-built changing room; far enough from the furnace to preclude the need for fireproof stone construction. Walking eastwards you are presented with a choice; the room opening to the left was a hot, dry room, used prior to a cold plunge in the pool in the room opposite, to the right. Alternatively you could walk further on through a series of progressively warmer rooms leading to a hot pool at the far end, before returning for a final cold plunge.

The rooms were heated by means of an elaborate underfloor heating system, known as a hypocaust, which led hot air from the furnace under the stone flagging of the raised floor. The remains of the system can be seen in several of the bath-house rooms.

In from the cold

The whole experience would have been treated as an occasion for socialising and recreation as well as hygiene. Doubtless the warmth and familiarity of the bathing rituals would have been a considerable comfort to those stationed far from home on this remote and draughty fringe of the Empire.

73 A stone head of the goddess Fortuna
from Bearsden bath-house

CRAMOND, CITY OF EDINBURGH (76)
MIXTURE OF LOCAL AUTHORITY AND PRIVATE OWNERSHIP
NT 189 769

How to get there
Park at the large public car park on the right just before you reach the harbour
at Cramond. Walk back along the road and take the first left through the gate in
the stone wall to reach the area of the excavated buildings.

A Roman port?
At the other end of the Antonine Wall from Bearsden, but similarly encumbered
by modern buildings, is the fort of Cramond. This is thought to have been the
site of an important harbour, servicing the garrison on the Antonine Wall.

Figures from the mud
Some of the excavated stone buildings within the fort have been laid out by
the local authority, including the headquarters building and granaries. The site is
probably most celebrated now, however, as the find-spot of a remarkable statue
of a lioness devouring a hapless male figure, found eroding from the harbour
muds in 1997. Originally it was probably one of a pair guarding the tomb of a
prominent military figure. The statue can now be seen in the National Museums
of Scotland.

Although the visible buildings are most probably Antonine, Cramond is one of the few locations confidently ascribed to the latest Roman presence in Scotland, as pottery and coins of late date have been found here in reasonable quantities. It appears that the fort and harbour were used as a base by the army and navy of the Emperor Severus in his campaigns in the early third century AD presumably after several decades of abandonment.

8

Picts, Angles, Scots and Britons

By the time the Roman army finally abandoned Britain in the fifth century AD, the numerous Iron Age tribes of Scotland had consolidated into a series of disparate kingdoms, each following a stuttering and uncertain path towards political and social cohesion (74). The largest was the Pictish kingdom which had formed from a confederacy of earlier tribes. By the fifth century AD it apparently controlled Scotland north of the Forth and Clyde with the exception of Argyll. Perhaps because of its geographical extent and essentially tribal composition, the kingdom was never entirely stable and was prone to periodic swings of power between the leading families in different regions.

Argyll was the power base of a different kingdom whose history and destiny were intertwined with that of the Picts. This was the kingdom of Dalriada headed by families who claimed descent from Irish royalty. They were known as Scots (from Scotti, meaning Irish!), and their eventual union with the Picts, under kings of Dalriadic birth, led ultimately to the use of the name Scotland to refer to the whole combined territory (after a period when it was known as Alba).

South of the Forth, in the area of modern Lothian, was the territory of the Gododdin, descendants of the Iron Age Votadini, while in the west lay the kingdom of Strathclyde. Not yet present, but soon to become a major player in the politics and social geography of southern Scotland, was the Anglian kingdom of Northumbria.

All the various 'peoples' of fifth century Scotland were descendants of the Celtic-speaking Iron Age tribes who had resisted and ultimately ousted the Roman army in earlier centuries (the 'migration' of the Dalriadic Scots from Ireland, if it happened at all, was probably little more than the movement of a few powerful families). It is little surprise then that it can be hard to discern

74 Map of sites in Chapter 8

major differences in the archaeological remains left by people whose allegiance lay with distinct kingdoms. Aside from a few items of material culture that might have given conscious physical expression to concepts like Pictishness (notably the extraordinary Pictish symbol stones), life was lived in much the same way under each of these various dynasties (75).

Historical records of various kinds give us a more detailed framework for understanding in this period than is available for earlier times; hence the adoption of the term Early Historic for this period to replace the rather pejorative Dark Ages. Yet the records are sparse and deal only with the upper echelons of society; much remains to be gleaned from the archaeological remains.

DUNADD, ARGYLL (77)
HISTORIC SCOTLAND
NR 837 935

How to get there
The minor road to the hill is sign-posted from the A816 about 1 mile (1.5km) north of Kilmichael Glassary. Follow the footpath from the car park at the base of the slope.

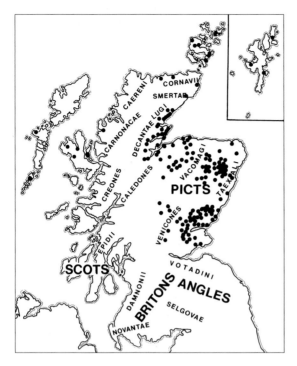

75 This map shows the spread
of Pictish symbol stones across
the parts of Scotland occupied
by the Picts: the names in
smaller typeface are the earlier
Iron Age tribes encountered
by the Roman army

The moss fortress

The hill of Dunadd is a remarkable natural fortress, set amidst a near flat valley
containing the Moine Mhor (the 'big moss'); part of the flood plain of the River
Add (*colour plate 21*). It has long been regarded as the principal centre of the Scots
of Dalriada. Excavations in the early part of the twentieth century, and again in
the 1980s, suggest that the hill was the site of an Iron Age fort long before the
emergence of Dalriada, but there are no standing remains that can be linked
unambiguously to that period. The site seems to have entered its most important
period of occupation during the sixth to ninth centuries AD.

The debris of fine-metal-working shows that a metal-smith's workshop was
based somewhere on the hill producing a range of goods, including elaborate
brooches, for the Dalriadic hierarchy. Metal-working of such a high calibre seems
to have been more or less restricted to the strongholds of the social elite, whose
patronage enabled the smiths to work at their craft full-time.

Steps to the top

As you climb the hill you pass through a series of ascending walled terraces (*76*).
To enter the first of these you must pass along a narrow natural cleft in the rock,
which would originally have been guarded by timber entrance-works. This first
terrace was once scattered with rectangular buildings, but little is now visible,
although the thick drystone wall around the terrace edge is well-preserved. Well-

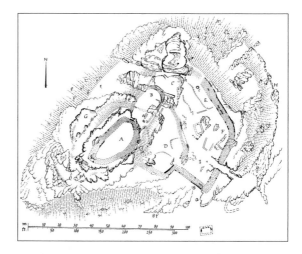

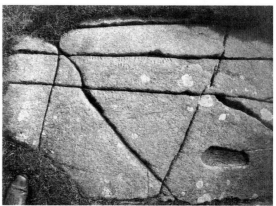

76 This schematic plan shows the nucleated nature of the fort of Dunadd, Argyll. The accompanying photograph shows the hollowed-out footprint carved into the summit of Dunadd, and the ogam inscription which accompanies it

worn paths lead up through further terraces to the summit, where the top two enclosures are noticeably more stoutly-walled than those below.

A hilltop hierarchy

It seems that the builders of terraced or 'nuclear' forts such as Dunadd made deliberate use of the naturally stacked terraces to separate different groups of people and activities, perhaps grading them according to status. Thus, at the summit of the fort was the citadel, the highly defended inner sanctum; presumably the seat of the petty kings for whom Dunadd was a principal power base. Irish documents of the same broad period give very precise instructions for the laying out of lordly residences, and social standing could be marked by one's physical proximity to the lord's own residence. Similar mechanisms may well have been in play at sites like Dunadd.

Between earth and sky

Perhaps the most peculiar characteristic of the fort, however, is the extraordinary series of carvings which can be found on an outcrop of rock on the lower of the two summit enclosures (those on view are fibre-glass replicas). These include a boar, carved in a similar style to the Pictish symbol stones (see below), a hollow basin and an unintelligible inscription in a form of writing known as ogam (where words are formed by a groups of vertical strokes).

Best of all, however, are the shallow carved impressions of two outsized human feet. Such carvings are thought to have been associated with inauguration rituals of Early Historic kings before Christianity robbed kingship of its supernatural pagan trappings (see also the similar stone at Clickhimin broch tower, Chapter 6). The use of such pagan symbols may, of course, have been carried through into the Christian period by force of tradition. It seems, then, that not only was Dunadd a key power centre in Dalriada, but perhaps the place where the first Dalriadic kings were inaugurated.

Seats of power

Strongholds like Dunadd would have served many functions. Perhaps primarily they were defensible residences and visible symbols of lordly or kingly power. They also served as a base for the ruler's retinue; warriors, advisors, craftsmen, and assorted hangers-on. They were places in which the tribute owed by the surrounding population could be collected, where guests could entertained and patronage dispensed, where judgements could be made and sentences passed.

The transactions conducted at such centres were not merely between ruler and subject. Dunadd has yielded fragments of pottery vessels imported from mainland Europe, including containers for wine and dye. Adomnan's Life of Columba describes how, in the sixth century AD, the saint met sailors from Gaul at the 'chief place in the region'; almost certainly Dunadd. An astonishing assortment of people, including merchants, sailors, clerics and warrior-potentates, seems to have mingled within this fortress at the height of Dalriada's power.

DUNDURN, PERTHSHIRE (78)
PRIVATE OWNERSHIP
NN 707 233

How to get there

From the eastern end of St Fillans, cross the bridge over the Earn and take the turning for Wester Dundurn. Pass the farm, heading for St Fillan's Chapel and approach the hill (which will by now be fairly obvious) via its north-west flank. You should ask permission at the farm before entering.

77 Dundurn, Perthshire

A front-line fort

In many ways the Pictish fort of Dundurn is rather similar to its Dalriadic counterpart of Dunadd. Like its western cousin, Dundurn occupies a site of great natural strength, a steep-sided rocky knoll set in a commanding physical location overlooking a hefty swathe of the rich farmlands of Strathearn (*77*). This valley, stretching westwards into the Highland massif, formed a prime route-way from east to west, linking the combative kingdoms of Pictland and Dalriada. As such it was an important place from which to launch or block incursions by raiding parties or armies from either side.

The path to summit crosses a series of natural but artificially enhanced terraces, edged by the tumbled remains of stone walls. These lead eventually to a small, but heavily defended, stone-walled summit. Excavation of this uppermost enclosure showed that a massive stone wall, 4m thick and with a skeleton of timbers held together with iron nails, enclosed an area some 20m by 15m. It is impossible to be sure whether this was a single roofed building, or whether it simply encircled a series of timber lean-to structures. Sealed beneath it lie the foundations of an earlier timber enclosure.

The overall plan of the fort is a bewildering mass of interlocking enclosures, crags and terraces, measuring over 300m by almost 200m. Much of the interior, however, would probably have been too rocky and irregular for building. The fort seems to have evolved over many years, with extra enclosures being added as needs changed and as the size of the resident population fluctuated.

Finds of silver and glass from the hilltop, and a finely decorated leather shoe, provide archaeological confirmation of activity in the fort in the Early Historic period, and presumably point to inhabitants of some rank and wealth. Roman masonry built into the citadel may represent another flourish of ostentation rather than opportunistic re-use of material, for it probably had to brought some distance to the hilltop.

One particularly fine glass boss seems to have been intended as an adornment for a reliquary (containing the remains of a saint) or perhaps a chalice. Evidence for the manufacture of fine jewellery seems to confirm also the presence of craftsmen on the hill, presumably specialists operating under the authority and patronage of the local ruler.

Citadels under siege

Like Dunadd, the stronghold of Dundurn found its way into the limited surviving literature of Early Historic Scotland. A record in the Annals of Ulster (probably written in Iona) mentions sieges of both Dunadd and Dundurn in AD 683, suggesting fairly major military operations in this period (although the Annals are characteristically unforthcoming as to who was besieging and who was defending in each case).

There seems little doubt that this was a place of some political, military and symbolic importance; an outpost of the Pictish kingdom entrusted to a regional potentate or sub-king on the front line in the rumbling, centuries-long conflict with Dalriada. After the merging of the two kingdoms in the ninth century AD, there was no longer much need for this borderland fort, and it was seemingly abandoned around the turn of the millennium.

DUMBARTON ROCK, WEST DUNBARTONSHIRE (79)
HISTORIC SCOTLAND
NS 400 744

How to get there
The site is sign-posted from the A82 south of Dumbarton town centre.

Fortress of the Britons
Early historical records mention Alt Cluith (or Clyde Rock), a stronghold of the Britons of Strathclyde, which was periodically attacked and besieged between the fifth and tenth centuries AD. The site has been unambiguously linked with Dumbarton Rock, on the north bank of the Clyde where it meets the River Leven, west of

Glasgow. It seems more than likely that this fort was as important to the Britons of Strathclyde as Dunadd was to the Scots of Dalriada.

Most of the visible remains on Dumbarton Rock are much later in date than the Early Historic fort; indeed, most are from the sixteenth century and later. The only known early defence (barely visible today) is a timber and rubble bank overlooking the isthmus which links the hill to the shore. Nonetheless, it is easy to appreciate the dominance of the site; a great plug of basalt, set on the Firth of Clyde close to its lowest crossing point (prior to dredging). From this elevated vantage point the kings of Strathclyde commanded the natural access routes into west-central Scotland, the heartland of their kingdom.

Debris of lordship

Excavations during the 1980s confirmed the historical evidence for occupation in the Early Historic period, uncovering finds including imported pottery and glass dating to the sixth to ninth centuries AD. Two carved stones dating to this period can also be seen in the Governor's House. A Viking raid attested in the Annals of Ulster around AD 870 may finally have brought the British occupation of the hill to an end. Yet such was the strategic importance of the site that it remained in use as a fortification until recent times.

DALMAHOY, MIDLOTHIAN (80)
PRIVATE OWNERSHIP
NT 135 669

How to get there

Take the minor road south from the A71 at Burnwynd, around 3 miles (5km) east of Livingston. Turn right at the T-junction and cross the railway bridge. Dalmahoy Hill and Kaimes Hill are clearly visible to the south. Dalmahoy Hill is best approached along the track between the two, which takes you around the base of the hill to its south-west flank.

A Lothian fortress

Another nuclear fort, though one which has never been excavated, lies on Dalmahoy Hill, west of Edinburgh. Approaching the hill from its south-western flank, you pass through a series of walled terraces, some edged by fairly massive stone slabs. On the summit, as at Dunadd and Dundurn, is a thick-walled citadel, commanding extensive views over the Midlothian countryside, and north to Fife. Despite the lack of excavation, surface finds of Early Historic metalwork suggest that Dalmahoy Hill may well have been a stronghold of the Gododdin.

MOTE OF MARK, DUMFRIES AND GALLOWAY (81)
NATIONAL TRUST FOR SCOTLAND
NX 845 540

How to get there

Take the minor road to Rockcliffe from the A710 around 4½ miles (7km) south-east of Dalbeattie. A sign-posted path, around ¼ mile (0.5km) long, leads to the site from the north end of the village.

Kingdom of the south-west

From what we know of the political geography of Early Historic Scotland, the Mote of Mark lay in the kingdom of Rheged, a Celtic-speaking state based in the south-west. The fortified hilltop overlooks the estuary of the River Urr, and excavation has shown that it was occupied between the fifth and seventh centuries AD.

During this period a truly massive timber-laced wall surrounded the twin summits, with an inner wall of slightly lesser dimensions. When in use, the outer wall was probably some 3m high by 3m wide. Eventually it was burnt down, probably by Northumbrian invaders, in heat so intense that much of the stone melted and fused into glassy lumps.

Well-connected rulers

As at Dunadd and elsewhere, there is evidence that fine metal-working was carried out within the confines of the fort, presumably under the patronage of a local Rheged warlord. Fragments of Gaulish pottery and decorated glass from the Rhineland hint at the connections enjoyed by the local nobility.

BURGHEAD, MORAY (82)
PRIVATE OWNERSHIP AND HISTORIC SCOTLAND (WELL ONLY)
NJ 109 691 (FORT), NJ 110 691 (WELL)

How to get there

The coastal village of Burghead is some 7 miles (11km) north-west of Elgin. The fort partly underlies the village, but some parts are preserved on the promontory beyond the modern houses.

War at sea

Much of the fighting between the warring states of Early Historic Scotland would have taken place at sea. One record mentions the wrecking of 150 Pictish ships in AD 729, suggesting that the Picts at least had a navy of some size. These boats were probably crewed by around 20 individuals. Some may have been

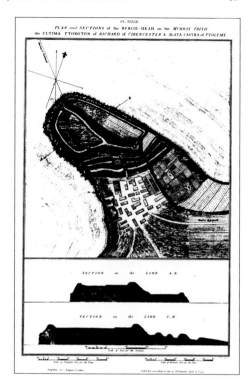

78 This early plan shows the remains of
the fort at Burghead in 1793

skin-covered 'currachs' although there are documentary references to timber-
built boats with mast and sail. Clearly, then, we should expect to find coastal
fortifications where this navy may have been based.

A Pictish naval base

The best candidate for a Pictish naval stronghold is Burghead, where early plans
depict multiple ramparts sealing off the promontory. Unfortunately the building of
the nineteenth-century planned village destroyed most of these defences (*78*). Yet
the finds from the site (notably around 30 stones carved with Pictish bull symbols)
and the scale of the surviving defences suggest that Burghead would have been
a major centre during this period. Aside from the citadel at Dundurn (see above)
Burghead is also the only known site of this period in Britain where iron nails
were used to join timbers in the ramparts; a sign of considerable wealth. Indeed, it
is not impossible that Burghead was a royal fortress visited or occupied by Pictish
kings.

Fragments of a fortress

Beyond the village, the promontory lies at two distinct levels. The upper was
the citadel of the original fort separated by a grassed-over wall from the lower
ward. In the latter, limited excavations demonstrated the presence of numerous

early buildings. The other survival from the fort's nineteenth-century destruction is an elaborate stone well or tank, set within a rock-cut chamber. This is now surrounded by modern houses, but would once have lain inside the fort. The key can be collected locally.

DOON HILL, EAST LOTHIAN (83)
HISTORIC SCOTLAND
NT 686 755

How to get there
The approach to Doon Hill is sign-posted from the A1 a few miles south of Dunbar. A lengthy unmetalled farm track leads up the hill to the site.

Kingdoms at war
During the seventh century AD, a wholly new political and military power forced it way into southern Scotland. This was the Anglian kingdom of Northumbria which gained the lands that now form Lothian and the Borders, from the ailing kingdom of Gododdin. A major centre of this period now underlies the town of Dunbar, and other traces of Northumbrian settlement are preserved in nearby place-names like Tyninghame and Whittinghame (the suffix '-hame' relating to late seventh- and eighth-century Northumbrian settlement). One of the few visible remnants of this Northumbrian conquest, however, is preserved on the upper slopes Doon Hill, a hillside location that gives fine views over the coastal plain to the east.

Overlapping halls
Excavations on Doon Hill during the 1960s revealed the remains of two successive timber halls. The outlines of both, and the enclosure in which they stood, have since been laid out in colour-coded concrete to give an idea of the form and scale of the buildings. A series of seemingly earlier burial remains are also marked out, but their relationship to the halls is unclear.

The surrounding polygonal enclosure would have formed a secure barrier around the main accommodation. It was formed of split timbers, set in a trench, with a continuous fence running between them. Inside, in the first phase, stood a massive timber hall, some 23m long. The building had been maintained for some time, and had been subject to periodic repair. Posts inside divided it into three chambers, the middle one being by far the largest, and probably the scene of lordly feasting and associated excesses. This first hall is thought, largely on the basis of its date, to have belonged to a warlord of the native Gododdin.

Feasting halls

Early Welsh literature preserves an evocative account of the heroic Celtic society of the period in the collection of poems known as Y Gododdin, thought to be the work of the sixth-century British poet Aneirin. This work comprises a series of elegies for the fallen heroes of the Gododdin, slain by the Northumbrians at the Battle of Catraeth (probably Catterick) at around the time when Doon Hill was occupied. The poems describe the year-long feast held at Din Eidyn (Edinburgh Castle Rock) prior to the campaign.

Y Gododdin recounts that much mead and wine was quaffed from fine glass vessels and elaborate drinking horns, and mention is made of the sumptuous furnishings of the 'splendid hall', even including 'feather cushions'. Although perhaps rather exaggerated, Aneirin's description gives a flavour of the warrior ethos of the society in which the Doon Hill hall was built and occupied.

Destruction and rebuilding

After the destruction of this first hall by fire, a second version was built to a rather different plan. It was still, however, a massive rectangular building. Close similarities with a Northumbrian hall at Yeavering in Northumberland, suggest that it was probably built around AD 640. Since the Gododdin stronghold of Din Eidyn was taken by the Northumbrian army in AD 638, it seems more than likely that the second hall on Doon Hill was the seat of one of the new Northumbrian rulers.

BOSTA, LEWIS, WESTERN ISLES (84)
PRIVATE OWNERSHIP
NB 136 403

How to get there

Drive to the north end of Great Bernera, through the township of Bosta, following the signs 'to the shore'. From the small car-park at the end of the road, walk around the seaward end of the cemetery to the small, fenced enclosure which contains the foundations of the excavated houses.

In search of the common people

So far, the sites in this chapter have been exclusively the defended homes of the social elite; the petty kings and potentates who dominated Early Historic Scotland through military force and the accrued wealth and prestige of their families. In contrast to the Iron Age, when the Scottish landscape was littered with the remains of farming settlements, the mass of the people of the post-Roman centuries, seem to have inhabited buildings that leave little archaeological trace.

A shift in power

One reason may be that power was now much more concentrated in fewer hands. Consequently, the lower orders may have had much less control over their own labour, and less access to building materials and other resources which might have enabled them to construct substantial houses. Where we do find buildings of this period, as in the Northern and Western Isles, they are generally built on a smaller scale than their Iron Age predecessors. Many such structures can be seen, for example, on the sites of earlier broch towers in Orkney (as at Gurness, see Chapter 6) and Shetland, although these have often suffered at the hands of antiquarian broch-hunters, digging in search of the earlier, more substantial buildings.

The dune village

The cluster of stone houses that forms the Early Historic period village of Bosta nestles in the dune slopes behind a wide expanse of sandy beach (79). The site was revealed during the early 1990s as the wind and tide gradually forced back the edge of the dunes, uncovering tumbled stonework and spreads of midden. Excavations in 1996 unveiled the remains of a remarkably well preserved series of houses dating to roughly the sixth to eighth centuries AD. The houses had to be largely dismantled, as there was no way of consolidating their fragile walls, but the foundations and lower wall courses have been preserved and laid out for the visitor.

The location, at the head of a sheltered bay, is a natural one for early settlement. Although only the latest phases of the settlement have been exposed, it is more than likely that this site was occupied for centuries, if not millennia, prior to the Early Historic period. A scatter of Viking finds and the fragmentary

79 Bosta, Lewis, Western Isles

remains of rectangular houses (now removed) suggest that the later periods of occupation have long since been lost to erosion.

Cellular houses

The Early Historic houses were of cellular form, and at least three or four appear to have been occupied at once. The buildings were built to a fairly regular plan, suggesting that strong social rules governed the layout. They were, however, far less monumental than their predecessors in the islands; the brochs and wheelhouses. The finds from the site are still being analysed at the time of writing, but the indications are that Bosta was essentially a village of farmers and fishermen.

The Northern and Western Isles seem, at this time, to have been part of the Pictish kingdom, but their location far from the centres of political power, suggests that their affiliations need not have been particularly strong. It is possible that the sea battles and sieges of the warring dynasties impacted little on the inhabitants of Bosta. Alternatively, however, it is a distinct possibility that men from the village owed duties of war service which, from time to time, may have led them far to the south and east.

ABERLEMNO, ANGUS (85)
HISTORIC SCOTLAND
NO 522 559

How to get there

The three stones are set up by the roadside in the village of Aberlemno on the B9134 between Forfar and Brechin. They are covered over in winter to protect them from the elements.

Mysterious Picts?

Little in Scottish archaeology has caught the popular imagination to the same extent as Pictish symbol stones (*colour plate 22*). Hundreds of standing stones, elaborately carved with a variety of mysterious and recurring motifs, can be found throughout the length and breadth of Pictland, from Orkney and the Western Isles south to the Forth. Few are found elsewhere. Clearly their meaning and purpose was well understood by the people who commissioned and carved them, and by their intended audience. There is no agreement today, however, as to the meaning of the symbols, and this, more than anything else, has contributed to the image of the Picts as a mysterious lost people.

A wealth of symbols

The symbols seem to date to the period from the sixth to ninth centuries AD, the heyday of the Pictish kingdom, prior to the union with Dalriada. Aside from the stones, themselves, the symbols are occasionally found elsewhere, on cave walls, architectural fragments, and on jewellery. There can be little doubt that their origins and distribution are intimately related to the establishment of the Pictish state.

Some of the symbols represent animals, birds and fish. Others depict objects such as mirrors and combs. Many, however, such as the crescent and V-rod, double discs, and the Z-rod, are much less obvious. These rather cumbersome terms used to describe the motifs, e.g. crescent and V-rod, are just simple descriptions of the shapes of the symbols.

When these stones were first erected it is highly likely that they would have been brightly painted and far more immediate in visual impact than they are today. Perhaps the best clues to their likely original appearance are in the decorative panels that adorn the pages of illuminated manuscripts of the same period.

Roadside stones

The three roadside stones at Aberlemno give an excellent introduction to the symbolic world of the Picts. The first was probably, in its original incarnation, a prehistoric standing stone, as it bears the faint traces of Neolithic or Bronze Age cup-marks on its reverse side. In the Pictish period, however, it was deeply incised with a double disc and Z-rod, and a mirror and comb. The mirror and comb motifs are almost always found together, and it has been suggested (though it is by no means proved) that they are female symbols, relating to the patron who had the stone carved, or to the person it commemorates. The next stone in line has simple decoration, restricted to a crescent and curved line. Both of these stones have been moved in recent times.

Images of Christianity

The final stone is much more elaborate; a carefully shaped slab, carved in relief rather than incised (see pl. 12). It seems to stand in its original position. Dominating the front face is a symbol that is far from Pictish in origin; the Christian cross. Although some early Pictish symbols stones include depictions of Christian motifs, overt Christian symbolism in Pictish art becomes dominant with the appearance of cross-slabs at the beginning of the eighth century.

Living symbols

The traditional symbols of the earlier stones by no means died out with the introduction of Christianity; numerous Pictish animals, objects and abstract symbols adorn the backs and sides of cross-slabs. The reverse of the roadside cross-slab at Aberlemno displays such symbols, including a vividly depicted hunting scene.

Carvers and patrons

Fine cross-slabs such as this were clearly the product of specialist stone-carvers, implying the presence of wealthy patrons; presumably from among the local nobility. The Aberlemno stones stand close to the Iron Age fort of Finavon, which may have continued as a Pictish centre. It is tempting to suggest that the inhabitants of the hilltop fort may have been the source of this patronage.

ABERLEMNO CHURCHYARD, ANGUS (86)
HISTORIC SCOTLAND
NO 522 555

How to get there

Take the minor road to the east just south of the roadside stones (above). This stone stands in the churchyard at the end of the road.

A battle remembered

This interlaced cross is carved in high relief, flanked by a series of animals, including two finely-carved sea-horses which face each other with forelegs raised. The reverse is even more extraordinary, however, for below a series of abstract symbols, it depicts several stages in a battle-scene involving mounted warriors and foot-soldiers (80).

It has been plausibly suggested that the slab depicts the nearby Battle of Nechtansmere, at which the Pictish army routed the Northumbrians in AD 685. Certainly the dating fits, and the cross slab might well have seemed an appropriate way to give thanks for a crucial Pictish victory, whilst simultaneously displaying the wealth and military muscle of the victors. On this basis, the mounted figure in the helmet with distinctive nose-guard would be the Northumbrian king Ecgfrith. The other mounted warrior would be the Pictish king Bridei. The cartoon-like panels show unfortunate Ecgfrith first fleeing, then turning to fight his pursuers, and eventually being killed and eaten by ravens.

DUNFALLANDY, PERTHSHIRE (87)
HISTORIC SCOTLAND
NN 946 565

How to get there

Follow the signs to Dunfallandy from Pitlochry. Park by the cattle grid just past the Dunfallandy Hotel. The stone stands at the top of a steep flight of steps which also lead to the cemetery.

Left: 80 The battle-scene on the rear of the Aberlemno Churchyard stone, Angus

Opposite: 81 The Pictish stone at Eassie, Angus; from a drawing first published by P. Chalmers in 1848

A Pictish beast

The sharp relief of this cross-slab and the vigour of its carving make it an impressive sight, despite its encasement in a protective glass shelter. On one side is a great cross, flanked by depictions of angels and animals. On the reverse is a wealth of Pictish symbols, including a double disc, and a crescent and V-rod.

One symbol of particular note is the so-called 'Pictish beast' (or 'swimming elephant'), which is found on numerous symbol stones. Unlike the usual naturalistic Pictish animals this peculiar creature may represent a fantastical animal, or may be an imaginative mis-rendering of a dolphin, porpoise, or even elephant.

EASSIE, ANGUS (88)
HISTORIC SCOTLAND
NO 352 474

How to get there

Eassie old church is sign-posted by the side of the A94 between Glamis and Coupar Angus. The stone stands within the roofless church.

A Pictish figure

Although this, like Dunfallandy, is an impressive Christian cross-slab, the stone is most notable for its fine depiction of a Pictish warrior beside the cross on the

PLATE XVI.

front face (*81*). The man is cloaked and carries a long spear and a small square shield. The presence on the same face of a stag may indicate that the figure is equipped for hunting rather than for war.

MEIGLE, ANGUS (89)
HISTORIC SCOTLAND
NO 287 445

How to get there
Meigle lies on the A94 between Perth and Forfar. The museum is in the centre of the village.

A gallery of symbols
The sheer wealth of stone sculpture from Meigle suggests that this was an important ecclesiastical centre from at least the ninth century AD. A collection of around 30 stones, dominated by Christian monuments, is housed in a small museum. Earlier Pictish symbol stones are apparently absent.

As well as conventional Pictish motifs, such as Pictish beasts, mirror and comb symbols, and Z-rods, the stones include several depictions of people, including horsemen. Among the Christian motifs is a depiction, on one cross-slab, of Daniel flanked by lions.

ST VIGEANS, ANGUS (90)
HISTORIC SCOTLAND
NO 638 429

How to get there

The stones are housed in a small museum sign-posted from the A933 between Arbroath and Friockheim. The key can be obtained locally.

Fragments of a church

St Vigeans takes it names from the seventh-century Irish saint Vigianus. Although nothing survives of the earliest church, the substantial collection of Pictish stones recovered from the site during building works in the nineteenth century, suggests that a church stood here as early as the ninth century AD. Among the stones, which are mostly pieces of cross-slabs, are some decorated architectural fragments of this early church.

DUNROBIN CASTLE, SUTHERLAND (91)
PRIVATE OWNERSHIP
NC 850 008

How to get there

The Castle is on the east coast of Sutherland, just north of Golspie.

Sutherland stones

Almost all of the numerous symbol stones which have turned up along the east coast of Sutherland over the years have ended up in this small museum in the grounds of Dunrobin Castle. Particularly fine examples include a stone with an intricately carved salmon, a mirror and comb, and an odd symbol shaped like a tuning fork. Another is a large cross-slab with a multiplicity of figures and symbols on its reverse side, including a gnome-like man with an axe and short sword. This stone also has a rare, but unintelligible ogam inscription down one of its sides.

WEMYSS CAVES, FIFE (92)
PRIVATE OWNERSHIP
NT 342 969 (WEST END)

How to get there

Park in the village of East Wemyss and walk along the coast to the north-east. In turn you will pass the entrances to Court Cave, Doo Cave (which no longer has any visible symbols) and Jonathon's Cave (the most obvious). It is advisable to check with the local council over the accessibility of these caves. The caves further on are not recommended for visitors. Take a torch.

Cave carvings

Pictish symbols were not restricted to standing stones, and the walls of these caves on the Fife coast show them in a wholly different context. Sadly, erosion and vandalism have taken their toll, and the Pictish symbols, which include several animals and abstract motifs, are in some cases obscured by later additions and modern graffiti. Nonetheless, Jonathon's Cave in particular remains an evocative site, while a spear-wielding figure in the entrance to Court Cave is an unusual addition to the roster of Pictish human representations.

SUENO'S STONE, MORAY (93)
HISTORIC SCOTLAND
NJ 046 595

How to get there

The stone stands on the eastern fringe of Forres sign-posted from the B9011 Kinloss road. The stone is unmissable, encased in a towering glass box which was constructed to protect the fragile sandstone from further erosion. The generally sharp condition of the carving is probably a happy by-product of the fact that the stone lay buried for many centuries until its rediscovery in the eighteenth century.

A symbol of union?

This elegant monument, which takes it rather misleading name from Svein Forkbeard, an eleventh-century king of Denmark, aside from being the tallest piece of Early Historic sculpture in Scotland, is one of the most intriguing (*colour plate 23*). Although clearly in the Pictish style (albeit with strong Northumbrian influences), it lacks any trace of the enigmatic symbols. On the west face is a tall slender cross, while the reverse seems to commemorate a great battle. At the base of the cross is a scene seemingly showing the inauguration of a king. The monument most probably dates to within a century after the union of Pictland and Dalriada in AD 843.

The battle for Moray?

A series of panels on the east face depict scenes of fighting, and the decapitation of prisoners, in a cartoon-like style not dissimilar to that of the Aberlemno churchyard slab (see above). The effect, however, is much more formal, with massed ranks of foot-soldiers and cavalry arranged in rigidly defined horizontal panels (*82*). The effect lies somewhere between the Aberlemno stone and the Bayeux Tapestry.

Moray, in which Sueno's Stone stands, was a semi-independent bastion of the Pictish state and was to prove a troublesome province for the kings of Scots for several centuries after the union with Pictland. It may be that this stone commemorates a victory over the armies of Moray by a king of Scots; perhaps Kenneth MacAlpin or his successors. This seems more probable than the alternative theory that it shows a mythical battle, since it seems unlikely that the resources required to sculpt and erect this massive slab, some 6.5m high, would have been lavished on anything other than a monument of considerable political and symbolic importance. This may also explain why, an unknown time after its construction, the stone was taken down and deliberately buried.

RUTHWELL CROSS, DUMFRIES AND GALLOWAY (94)
HISTORIC SCOTLAND
NY 100 682

How to get there
The cross has been moved in recent times inside Ruthwell Parish Church, just off the B724 around 5½ miles (9km) west of Annan.

The spread of the cross
From around the second half of the first millennium AD, Christianity began to have an increasingly important influence on the early kingdoms of Scotland. The emergence of cross-slabs as the dominant form in Pictish art seems to signal the conversion of the Pictish aristocracy.

For the Picts and the Dalriadic Scots, Celtic Christianity spreading westwards from Ireland was the main source of influence. For the Northumbrians, Roman Christianity spread from the south. Everywhere, however, a close relationship was soon established between the early Church and secular rulers who provided land and patronage in return for divine endorsement of their earthly rule.

The Ruthwell cross is the finest surviving example of the art of the Northumbrian stone-carvers, who worked around the same time as their Pictish counterparts to the north. This example probably dates to the beginning of the eighth century AD. We know nothing of who commissioned it, or why, but it was clearly someone of considerable wealth and status.

The cross stands around 5.2m high, only slightly smaller than Sueno's Stone. Parts of the upper section have been replaced and patched, to repair damage inflicted during the Reformation. The four carved faces depict a range of biblical scenes, with occasional fragments of text in Old English and Latin. The Old English text seems to encompass an early version of poem known as the 'Dream

82 This detail from Sueno's Stone seems to show rows of decapitated prisoners, on the upper left of the picture

of the Rood' (or cross) in which the story of the crucifixion is told, with the cross itself as narrator.

WHITHORN, DUMFRIES AND GALLOWAY (95)
PART HISTORIC SCOTLAND, PART CHURCH OF SCOTLAND
NX 444 402

How to get there
The entrance to the visitor centre is sign-posted from the main road in the village of Whithorn.

The earliest Christians
Whithorn has some claim to being the earliest centre of Christianity in Scotland. It is thought to have been the place where St Ninian came as bishop to an already established Christian community in the early part of fifth century AD. Most of the visible remains date to the medieval period, although there are some surviving fragments from the Early Christian establishment.

The lost church
The earliest object from the site is a rough carved stone bearing the name Latinus, which can be seen, along with numerous other carved stones, in the small site

museum. This early memorial, dated to the fifth century, came from excavations under the medieval church; possibly from the buried site of the early stone church (known from documentary sources as Candida Casa; the White House).

Excavations since the mid-1980s (still ongoing at the time of writing) have uncovered the buried remains of numerous other buildings and graves, from the Northumbrian period of occupation through to later medieval times. The foundations of many of these structures have been laid out for the visitor.

9

The Vikings

Across much of Scotland, direct physical evidence of the Viking presence is elusive. Most of the settlement remains (at least the excavated ones) are concentrated in the northern isles (*83*). Despite intensive Viking settlement on the north and west mainland and in the Western Isles, it is only recently that much work has been done on unearthing the remains of their settlements. There are few sites in these areas as yet where the standing remains would merit a visit.

The most common finds of the period are graves, either isolated or in cemeteries. The earliest, pagan Viking graves are often richly furnished with fine grave goods, probably reflecting the status of the deceased in a highly stratified society. A Viking cemetery dating from the ninth or tenth centuries AD on Cnip Headland in Lewis, for example, included one woman buried in typical Viking clothes, with a range of personal jewellery, including two bronze brooches and a necklace, and numerous other belongings. Others had been buried with only a shroud.

BROUGH OF BIRSAY, ORKNEY (MAINLAND) (96)
HISTORIC SCOTLAND
HY 239 285

How to get there
The Brough of Birsay is a tidal island lying off the north-west coast of mainland Orkney. To find it, follow the track northwards from Birsay to the car park. From there the island can be reached on foot at low tide. The very fine symbol

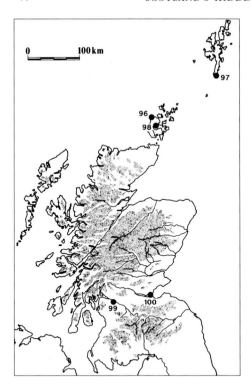

0 _____ 100 km

Left: 83 Map of sites in Chapter 9

Opposite: 84 This detail from a Pictish symbol stone from the Brough of Birsay seems to show a local ruler and his warrior retinue

stone found on the island is now in the National Museums of Scotland, but a replica has been installed on the site (*84*).

An island stronghold

Spread across the Brough of Birsay are the remains of numerous grassed-over building foundations, and the buried remains of many more houses, representing successive Pictish and Viking occupations of the island. Most of the visible house foundations belong to the Viking occupation, as does a small sandstone church dating to the twelfth century (*colour plate 24*).

Even before the Vikings arrived, the Brough of Birsay seems to have been a place of some importance. Numerous houses, a symbol stone depicting a king or chieftain and his retinue, and extensive debris from fine bronze-working, all suggest that the island was home to a substantial and prosperous Pictish community.

Consumers and producers

The island offered very limited resources for farming, being only some 50 acres (20ha) in extent, but the fertile land on the adjacent mainland appears to have been densely settled. Small farms, including one at Point of Buckquoy, just opposite the island, seem to have thrived here in the pre-Viking centuries. In all probability then, the Brough of Birsay was the seat of a local ruler, an island

equivalent of the Early Historic forts we saw in the previous chapter, drawing provisions and labour from subservient mainland farms.

The Viking take-over

The arrival of the Vikings at Birsay seems to have been heralded by a more or less complete annexation of both the existing power centre and its dependent farms. At Point of Buckquoy, new rectangular Viking houses were built directly over the ruins of their cellular Pictish predecessors, but the economy of the farm seems to have carried on much as before. A rash of characteristic Viking hall-houses (described in more detail at Jarlshof, below) sprang up on the island itself, and the remains of some can be seen upslope from the foundations of the church.

Colonisation or assimilation?

This transformation in building styles would seem to signal the commandeering of the island power base and the surrounding farmland by new people, at least at the top of the social scale. It is thus consistent with the traditional blood and guts view of the Viking take-over, where the hapless Picts were either driven out or put to the sword. A more detailed perusal of the results of excavation, however, reveals a rather different picture.

The radical change in building form, from cellular sprawl to rigid rectangle, must have entailed quite dramatic alterations in the way in which life was lived within the houses at Birsay. The changes in the allocation of space to different people, and to different activities, would have altered perceptions of social life and social relationships.

Yet other aspects of Pictish culture seem to have carried on with little obvious disruption. The 'Viking' farmers at Point of Buckquoy continued to use much the same set of tools and, more peculiarly, favoured the same range of personal items, including decorative pins, combs and other ornaments as their Pictish predecessors. Although the power centres and ownership of land may have passed to Viking hands, it is debatable how much change there was in the make-up of the population overall. We should not underestimate the speed and whole-heartedness with which the lower levels in society, presumably those with a long native pedigree, might have adapted to new ways of living which may have fitted the expectations of their new masters.

JARLSHOF, SHETLAND (MAINLAND) (97)
HISTORIC SCOTLAND
HU 398 095

How to get there
See entry in Chapter 6, where the prehistoric settlement at Jarlshof is also described.

Viking farmers
As well as being one of the key prehistoric settlements in Shetland, Jarlshof was the site of a long-lived Norse farm, first established by a Viking family in the ninth century AD (*colour plate 25*). In contrast to the Brough of Birsay, and despite the wealth of pre-Norse remains, there is little evidence of a preceding Pictish farm: it may lie largely under the hefty remains of the medieval farm and laird's house that occupy a major chunk of the site today. Also unlike Birsay, Jarlshof, despite its name, was probably not a settlement of any great consequence in the Viking period, other than within the immediate locality: it was almost certainly not the home of a Norse jarl.

The evolving farm
The maze of rectilinear buildings laid out before the visitor today comprise several centuries of the growth and modification of what was probably never more than a small homestead with one or two main houses and a set of associated barns and byres.

The first main house was of a distinctive Viking form (*85*). The interior was essentially a long rectangular chamber, entered via one of two opposing doors,

85 This artist's reconstruction shows a Viking longhouse similar to those found at Jarlshof

with timber benches drawn along both sides and a long hearth occupying the middle of the earthen floor. The whole interior of the house, some 20m by 5m was one great open space, apart from a cooking area screened off at one end. This was a house of quite respectable size which may well have accommodated a sizeable number of individuals, probably forming an extended family group. The exterior, too, may well have been somewhat different from earlier Pictish buildings, with a long ridged timber-framed roof, instead of the conical roofs of earlier roundhouses and cells.

Over time the farm changed its form to some degree. Outbuildings, including what seems to have been a smithy, came and went, and new houses replaced the old hall-house, which probably remained in use as an outbuilding. One outbuilding of particular interest is a small roughly square structure, the interior of which is occupied by a sizeable hearth. Such structures have sometimes been interpreted as saunas, where steam would be created by pouring water over hot stones in the hearth.

In the later period, the main house included within its walls an area for the stalling of livestock. This would have provided shelter for the animals as well as extra warmth for the inhabitants, and is an early example of the byre-house concept that was to persist in the Highlands and Islands into recent centuries.

Pictish graffiti

Most of the artefacts found within the farm were the mundane products of an agricultural economy, locally produced within a fairly self sufficient community.

A few bronze items, such as pins, may have come from further afield, and a fitting from the end of a leather strap was of a type usually found in Scandinavia. The most intriguing set of finds however were a series of rough carvings, including human heads and boats. The former were clearly executed in the same style as on Pictish symbol stones, right down to the hair styles and beards. No matter how massive were the social changes wrought in Shetland by the Vikings, the native Picts were far from obliterated and may have lived on even on sites as stereotypically 'Viking' as Jarlshof.

MAES HOWE, ORKNEY (MAINLAND) (98)
HISTORIC SCOTLAND
HY 318 127

How to get there
See entry in Chapter 3, where the Neolithic chambered tomb at Maes Howe is described.

The Vikings were here
The great burial mound of Maes Howe is well known as perhaps the finest chambered tomb in the country (see Chapter 3). But the tomb also houses one of the most unusual sets of Viking remains to be seen anywhere in Scotland: a series of about thirty inscriptions, carved in Viking runes, as well as carefully etched depictions of animals including a dragon and walrus (86).

The re-born tomb
Radiocarbon dates from the enclosing ditch and bank around the tomb suggest that it was re-used in the ninth century AD, shortly after the Viking incursions into Orkney. It seems likely that the great Neolithic mound, dormant for thousands of years, was pressed back into service as the burial place of a Viking lord. Any remaining Neolithic skeletons or grave goods were presumably removed at to make way for the new occupant.

Viking messages
The carved runic inscriptions, the largest collection to be seen in Scotland, are rather later in date than this presumed Viking burial, and probably date to the twelfth century AD. Some were apparently carved by a group of crusaders, gathering in the winter of 1153-4. Others were made at various times in the same general period.

The curse of the tomb?
At around the same time, Maes Howe appears in the Orkneyinga Saga as the mound of 'Orkahaugr' in which Earl Harald and his men sheltered from a

86 A carved Norse dragon from Maes
Howe, Orkney

snowstorm. It was perhaps on occasions such as this that many of the runes were
carved. As they waited, two of the Earl's followers are said to have gone mad: the
old tomb was clearly a place of some power to superstitious Vikings.

Missing treasure

Several inscriptions mention the former presence of a great treasure in the
mound, presumably Viking gold and silver, rather than crumbling Neolithic pots.
One inscription reads 'Hakon alone bore the treasure out of this mound' and
others elaborate the theme. Their position, at various points on the walls, shows
that the interior was largely empty once again: presumably the Viking burial had
by now been looted and the tomb once more cleared out.

GOVAN, GLASGOW (99)
CHURCH OF SCOTLAND
NS 553 658

How to get there

This extraordinary collection of Early Christian gravestones is kept in the Old
Parish Church in the centre of Govan, on the north side of Govan Road. Around
40 stones were moved into the church from the graveyard in the 1920s. Several
date as early as the tenth century AD.

Vikings further south

Although the visible remains of Viking settlements tend to be restricted to the far north and west, Viking raiders, farmers and traders settled in many other parts of Scotland and northern England. One of the few accessible traces of these southern Vikings are the distinctive stone grave markers known as hogback stones. Five good examples can be seen in the Old Parish Church at Govan in Glasgow, along with numerous other Early Christian crosses and grave-stones of slightly later date (another can be seen in the Historic Scotland museum at Meigle in Angus, see Chapter 8).

Hogbacks probably originated in northern England or southern Scotland some time in the tenth century, and were subsequently adopted further afield. A few are known from the northern and Western Isles, but they never seem to have found favour in the Scandinavian Viking homelands.

Dwellings of the dead

Hogback stones represented idealised houses. They derive their name from their high arching tops, which mimic the curving ridge poles of the house roof. Like excavated Viking buildings, the basic shape of hogbacks was rectangular. The carving on the upper parts of the stones usually mimicked the patterns of tiled roofs, while the ends (the 'gables' of the house) are decorated with animal motifs. Although the basic shape is reminiscent of the Jarlshof hall-houses, hogbacks may well represent mythical dwellings of the dead rather than any attempt to replicate domestic reality.

INCHCOLM, FIFE (100)
HISTORIC SCOTLAND
NT 189826

How to get there

The island of Inchcolm in the Firth of Forth can be reached by tourist ferry from South Queensferry, (or by boat from Burntisland if arranged in advance).

The abbey stone

Inchcolm island is the location of a well-preserved twelfth-century abbey, and various other remains which lie outside the chronological scope of this book (they are, of course, well worth a visit in their own right). Of more relevance here, however, is a particularly fine hogback stone which has recently been moved into the abbey church to protect it from the elements (87). This and other remains suggest that a religious community lived on the island many centuries before the building of the abbey.

Several rows of roof-tiles are clearly depicted along the body of the stone, with the heads of fierce-looking beasts peering out from either end. This particular

87 The hogback stone on Inchcolm

hogback is thought to be among the earliest found in Scotland, dating to the middle of the tenth century AD.

Christian or pagan?

Hogback stones probably covered the graves of Christian Vikings rather than the first pagan arrivals. The Inchcolm example was presumably originally employed in a burial ground belonging to the island's Christian community. After all, they are not too far removed in concept from Early Christian house-shrines, small reliquaries formed in the shape of rectangular houses. So far, none have been excavated in their original locations, so it we cannot be sure what form the rest of the burial rite took. No burials were found in situ under the Inchcolm stone when it was excavated prior to being moved inside the church.

The living and the dead

Whatever the origins of hogback stones, it is perhaps apt that we end this exploration of Scotland's monuments with a burial rite based around the motif of houses. Though very different in expression, the concept is strikingly reminiscent of the chambered tombs of the Neolithic, where burial also took place in houses of the dead; morbid reflections of the rather more transient homes of the living.

Museums to visit

By far the largest and most comprehensive collection of material relating to the archaeology of Scotland can be seen in the Museum of Scotland, Chambers St, Edinburgh. A number of other museums around the country have good displays of prehistoric and Early Historic material. These include:

Aberdeen, Anthropological Museum
Argyll, Kilmartin House Museum
Dumfries Museum
Dundee, McManus Galleries
Edinburgh, Huntly House Museum
Elgin Museum
Falkirk Museum
Forfar, Methan Institute
Glasgow Art Gallery and Museum
Glasgow, Hunterian Museum
Inverness Museum
Inverurie, Carnegie Museum
Islay, Museum of Islay Life, Port Charlotte
Kilmarnock, Dick Institute
Kirkcaldy Museum
Kirkcudbright, Stewartry Museum
Kirkintilloch Museum
Lewis, Museum nan Eilean, Stornoway
Montrose Museum

Orkney, Tankerness House Museum, Kirkwall
Perth Museum and Art Gallery
Rosemarkie, Groam House Museum
Rothesay, Bute Museum
Shetland, Lerwick Museum
Stirling, Smith Art Gallery and Museum
Thurso Heritage Museum

Several other museums hold substantial collections of Pictish stones:

Dunrobin Castle, Sutherland
Meigle, Angus
St Andrews Cathedral, Fife
St Vigeans, Angus

Other places to visit include reconstructions of prehistoric buildings:

Archaeolink Centre, Aberdeenshire (reconstructed Iron Age buildings)
Kenmore, Loch Tay, Perthshire (reconstructed crannog)

Further reading

SCOTTISH ARCHAEOLOGY — GENERAL

Edwards, K and Ralston, IBM (eds) 2003 *Scotland After the Ice Age: Environment, Archaeology and History, 8000 BC - AD 1000* (Edinburgh University Press).

Ritchie, A and Ritchie, JNG 1981 *Scotland: archaeology and early history* (Edinburgh University Press).

REGIONAL WORKS

The series of regional guides 'Exploring Scotland's Heritage', published by HMSO, is probably the best available for finding your way round the sites of all periods within any given part of Scotland. For many parts of the country there are weighty inventories of monuments published over many decades by the Royal Commission on the Ancient and Historical Monuments of Scotland (HMSO). The following books provide more general summaries for specific regions:

Armit, I 1996 *The Archaeology of Skye and the Western Isles* (Edinburgh University Press).

Fojut, N and Pringle, D 1993 *The ancient monuments of Shetland* (HMSO, Edinburgh).

Fojut, N, Pringle, D, and Walker, B 1994 *The ancient monuments of the Western Isles* (HMSO, Edinburgh).

Renfrew, AC (ed.) 1985 *The Prehistory of Orkney* (Edinburgh University Press).

Ritchie, A 1996 *Prehistoric Orkney* (Batsford, London).

Ritchie, JNG (ed.) 1997 *The Archaeology of Argyll* (Edinburgh University Press).

Turner, V 1998 *Ancient Shetland* (Batsford, London).

The chambered tombs of the north and west are unusually well-served in terms of guides, mainly thanks to the work of Audrey Henshall. The following publications are particularly useful:

Davidson, JL and Henshall AS 1989 *The chambered cairns of Orkney* (Edinburgh University Press).

Davidson, JL and Henshall AS 1991 *The chambered cairns of Caithness* (Edinburgh University Press).

Henshall, AS 1963 and 1972 *The chambered tombs of Scotland* (2 vols.) (Edinburgh University Press).

Henshall AS, and Ritchie, JNG 1995 *The chambered cairns of Sutherland* (Edinburgh University Press).

Henshall AS, and Ritchie, JNG 2001 *The chambered cairns of the Central Highlands* (Edinburgh University Press).

NEOLITHIC/BRONZE AGE

Ashmore, PJ 1995 *Calanais: the standing stones* (Urras nan Tursachan, Stornoway).

Ashmore, PJ 1996 *Neolithic and Bronze Age Scotland* (Batsford, London).

Barclay, GJ 1993 *Balfarg: the prehistoric ceremonial centre* (Fife Regional Council, Glenrothes).

Barclay, GJ 1998 *Farmers, Temples and Tombs* (Canongate, Edinburgh).

Burl, A 1995 *A guide to the stone circles of Britain, Ireland and Brittany* (Yale University Press, Newhaven and London).

Clarke, DV, Cowie, TG and Foxon, A 1985 *Symbols of Power at the time of Stonehenge* (National Museums of Scotland, Edinburgh).

Hedges, JW 1984 *Tomb of the Eagles* (John Murray, London).

IRON AGE

Armit, I (ed.) 1990 *Beyond the Brochs* (Edinburgh University Press).

Armit, I 2003 *Towers in the North: the Brochs of Scotland* (Tempus, Stroud).

Armit, I 2005 *Celtic Scotland: Iron Age Scotland in its European* Context (2nd edition: Batsford, London).

Armit, I and Fojut, N 1998 *Dun Charlabaigh and the Hebridean Iron Age* (Urras nan Tursachan, Stornoway).

Ballin-Smith, B and Banks, I (eds) 2002 *In the Shadow of the Brochs* (Tempus, Stroud).

Cunliffe, B 2004 *Iron Age Britain* (2nd edition, Batsford, London).

Dixon, N 2004 T*he Crannogs of Scotland: an Underwater Archaeology* (Tempus, Stroud).

Harding, DW, 2004 *The Iron Age in Northern Britain* (Routledge, London).

Hingley, R 1998 *Settlement and Sacrifice: the Later Prehistoric People of Scotland* (Canongate, Edinburgh).

Morrison, I 1985 *Landscape with Lake Dwellings* (Edinburgh University Press).

Ralston, IBM 2004 *The Hill-forts of Pictland since 'The Problem of the Picts'* (Groam House Museum, Rosemarkie).

ROMAN

Bishop, M (ed.) 2002 *Roman Inveresk: Past. Present and Future* (Armatura, Duns).

Breeze, DJ 1982 *The northern frontiers of Roman Britain* (Batsford, London).

Breeze, DJ 1996 *Roman Scotland* (Batsford, London).

Hanson, WS 1991 *Agricola and the Conquest of the North* (Batsford, London).

Hanson, WS and Maxwell, GS 1983 *Rome's North-West Frontier: the Antonine Wall* (Edinburgh University Press).

Keppie, L 2004 *The Legacy of Rome: Scotland's Roman Remains* (John Donald, Edinburgh).

Maxwell, GS 1990 *A battle lost: Romans and Caledonians at Mons Graupius* (Edinburgh University Press).

Maxwell, GS 1998 *A Gathering of Eagles* (Canongate, Edinburgh).

EARLY HISTORIC AND VIKINGS

Alcock, L 2003 *Kings and Warriors, Craftsmen and Priests in Northern Britain AD 550-850* (Society of Antiquaries, Edinburgh).

Campbell, E 1999 *Saints and Sea-Kings* (Canongate, Edinburgh).

Carver, M 1999 *Surviving in Symbols* (Canongate, Edinburgh).

Crawford, B 1987 *Scandinavian Scotland* (Leicester University Press).

Foster, SM 1996 *Picts, Gaels and Scots* (Batsford, London).

Graham-Campbell, G and Batey, CE, 1998 *Vikings in Scotland* (Edinburgh University Press).

Henderson, G and Henderson, I 2004 *The Art of the Picts: sculpture and metalwork in Early Medieval Scotland* (Thames and Hudson, London).

Hill, P 1997 *Whithorn and St Ninian* (Sutton, Stroud).

Lane, A and Campbell, E 2000 *Dunadd: an Early Dalriadic Capital* (Oxbow, Oxford).

Lowe, C 1999 *Angels, Fools and Tyrants* (Canongate, Edinburgh).

Mack, A 1997 *Field guide to the Pictish symbol stones* (Pinkfoot Press, Angus).

Owen, O 1999 *The Sea Road* (Canongate, Edinburgh).

Ritchie, A 1993 *Viking Scotland* (Batsford, London).

Ritchie, A (ed.) 1994 *Govan and its Early Medieval Sculpture* (Alan Sutton, London).

Ritchie, A 1997 *Iona* (Batsford, London).

Smyth, AP 1984 *Warlords and holy men: Scotland AD 80-1000* (Edinburgh University Press).

Glossary

barrow	A burial mound.
beaker	A type of Late Neolithic pottery vessel, usually highly decorated, found in many parts of north and west Europe.
broch / broch tower	A massive-walled stone roundhouse of tower-like proportions.
cists	A slab-lined grave pit, usually covered by a capstone. Basically a stone box.
crannog	An artificial islet, usually supporting a house.
cropmark	Marks in arable crops caused by the presence of buried archaeological sites. These are usually only visible from the air.
cup-marks	Decorative depressions carved into rock-faces of stone monuments, often arrayed in complex patterns.
dun	Derived from a Gaelic place-name meaning 'fort', this term is now a catch-all for small, stone-built roundhouses or enclosures.
henge	A type of circular enclosure formed by a ditch with an external bank. Thought to represent ritual monuments of the Later Neolithic period. Often have circles of stones or timbers inside.
hut circle	The remains of a prehistoric roundhouse, visible as a ring-shaped bank.
kerb	An edging of large stones set around, for example, a stone burial mound.
megalith	A rather archaic term used to refer to large stones used as standing stones or in the construction of major stone

monuments of the Neolithic period.

midden — A deposit of refuse or domestic rubbish.

monolith — A large single standing stone.

orthostat — An upright stone.

radiocarbon dating — A scientific method of dating organic objects, such as wood, bone or seeds.

palisade — A fence of close-spaced posts, usually set in a narrow trench packed with stones.

scarcement — A ledge projecting from the inner wall of a building, probably to help support a roof or floor.

souterrain — A semi-underground linear or curving chamber, probably used for the storage of grain and other produce.

wheelhouse — A stone roundhouse with a floor divided into a series of bays by stone piers resembling, in plan, the spokes of a wheel.

Index of sites